Shot

Bad Ass Outlaws, Gunmen, and Lawmen of the Old West

Copyright © 2016 / 2022 Nick Vulich

Table of Contents

Western Bad Men 1
   Joaquin Murrieta California Bandit 6
   Sam Bass – Texas Outlaw 11
   Jesse James and the James-Younger Gang 21
   Bob Ford – "The Dirty Little Coward" Who Shot Jesse James 28
   Rise and Fall of the Dalton Gang 34
   Black Bart – California's Gentleman Bandit, Stagecoach Robber, and PO8 41
   Belle Starr – Female Bandit of Indian Territory 48
   Tom "Black Jack" Ketchum 53
   Doolin-Dalton Gang, AKA The Wild Bunch 59
   "Dynamite Dick" Clifton – The "Most Killed Outlaw in the American West" 66
   Butch Cassidy and the Sundance Kid, AKA The Hole in the Wall Gang, AKA The Wild Bunch 74
   Pearl Hart - "The Lady Bandit" 85
Western Bad Men 91

Billy the Kid – New Mexico Outlaw, Gunfighter, and Cattle Thief 95

Luke Short – Frontier Scout, Gambler, and Gunfighter . 101

Gunfighter John Wesley Hardin 108

Doc Holliday – Frontier Gambler, Gunfighter, Sometimes Lawman 116

Robert A. "Clay" Allison 124

Western Lawmen 131

Wild Bill – James Butler Hickok 134

Wyatt Earp – Frontier Lawman 141

"Bat" Masterson – This Western Lawman Outlived Them All 151

Tom Horn – Cattle Detective 165

Heck Thomas - Lawman Extraordinaire 173

Bill Tilghman – Frontier Lawman, Politician, and Movie Maker 181

Appendix 1: Gunfight at the O. K. Corral 188

Appendix 2: Methods of Gunfighters 195

Appendix 3: Four Bad Men Who Made a Specialty of Carrying Guns 204

Appendix 4: First Account of Coffeyville, Kansas Bank Raid by the Dalton Brothers 213

About This Book 232

About the Author 235

Bibliography 237

Western Bad Men

For over 150 years, the image of western bad men has thrilled readers and filled movie screens. Who hasn't heard of Jesse James, the Dalton Brothers, Black Bart, or Belle Starr? They are as much a part of American folklore as George Washington, Abraham Lincoln, and Theodore Roosevelt.

Something about the west brought out the best and the worst in humankind. The funny thing is, a cult following has developed around many of these bandits, making them out to be something they never were.

The legend that grew up around Joaquin Murrieta was that he was just a regular guy who moved from Mexico to California and tried to strike it rich during the gold rush. Instead, he discovered a big sign that read, "No Mexicans Allowed." His supporters say he was forced into a life of outlawry because of the Foreign Claim Tax. And then, to support that claim, a whole legend has been built up about how he stole from the rich and shared his wealth with poor Mexican families. The only problem is the facts don't support that interpretation. Murrieta and his gang of outlaws specialized in robbing poor Chinese immigrants. The only people they shared with were themselves.

People told the same stories about Jesse James. Legend has it Jesse only stole from wealthy bankers and railroad men. He could disappear into thin air after pulling a bank job or train robbery because he shared the booty with poor Missouri families. But, as with Murrieta, that probably never happened. Jesse James was a thief. He robbed stagecoaches, banks, trains, and you-name-it. And, as far as just robbing the rich, not so. During most of their train and stage robberies, the James-Younger Gang collected money and jewelry from passengers, as well as the booty from the express car.

Bob Ford is another interesting character. He was a gunfighter, a robber wannabe, who, along with his brother, Charlie, got into Jesse James's good graces, then shot him in the back. Ironically, he met the same fate in a Colorado dancehall several years later.

My personal favorite is Black Bart, the gentlemen robber of the west. Bart only robbed Wells Fargo stagecoaches and always asked the drivers to "Please throw down the box." Of course, he backed his request up with a double-barreled shotgun. Bart singlehandedly pulled twenty-eight stagecoach robberies over eight years without firing a shot. When he was caught, he served his time and disappeared completely off the radar.

And last but not least, there's Belle Starr, one of the most badass female robbers on record. Belle called her pistols her "babies" and ruled an outlaw kingdom based out of her home in Indian Territory. She lived by the gun, and she died by the gun.

As I look back on my childhood days, reading through the books of Max Brand and Zane Grey, and paging through a bazillion and one western magazines—*Real West, True West, Frontier Times, Westerner,* and more, and watching God knows how many westerns—*Gun Smoke,* Bonanza, and the *Wild, Wild West*—the outlaw life was almost always portrayed as a glamorous life, filled with loose women, blazing guns, and saddlebags overflowing with gold, silver, and greenbacks.

What a life!

The only thing is all the movies, books, and TV shows painted a distorted portrait of life in the old west. For example, James Dodsworth lived the outlaw life for six weeks while riding as a spy with the Doolin-Dalton Gang. He said the gang was constantly on the move. They rarely spent more than one night in any one place. Dalton and Doolin worried they'd end up like Jesse James—shot in the back.

The gang always posted at least one man on watch duty at night. The rest of the gang slept with Winchesters by their sides and pistols under their heads. Then, everyone was ready to spring into action at a moment's notice.

And, as for those saddlebags overflowing with riches, more often than not, they were like a Charlie Brown Halloween special—filled with rocks rather than gold.

Sometimes the gang would cut off the wrong car during a train robbery and ride away empty-handed. Sometimes a posse would chase them off a little too soon before they could grab their booty. Other times, it was slim pickings, and there was nothing to take.

The first train job the Dalton Gang pulled went totally awry. The expressman got away before they could convince him to open the safe, and in their haste to rob the Atlantic Express, the boys forgot to bring dynamite. Black Jack Ketchum and his gang made off with $100,000 in unsigned banknotes that were not readily cashed. Pearl Hart's fame rests on a single stagecoach robbery that netted her under $500 and several years in the caboose after her arrest.

The sad truth is most outlaws led a short life that ended either at the end of a rope or with a bullet in the brain. Only a lucky few survived into the new century—Frank James, Cole Younger, and Emmett Dalton, to name a few.

(**Authors Note**: Seven of these stories first appeared in my previous book, *History Bytes: 37 People, Places, and Events That Shaped American History*. Some have been rewritten for this book, others shamelessly copied. The rest of the stories are new to this volume. I hope you enjoy reading them as much as I enjoyed writing them.)

Joaquin Murrieta California Bandit

Most of what we know about Joaquin Murrieta is pure horse hockey. A California journalist, John Rollin Ridge (Yellow Bird), created the legend most people know as Joaquin Murrieta in his 1854 book, *The Life and Adventures of Joaquin Murieta*.

Ridge's book makes it appear that Murrieta was a modern-day Robin Hood forced into outlawry by racist whites. It says he turned to stealing horses, robbery, and murder—robbing the rich, and distributing his plunder among poor Mexican families.

The only problem is there's no evidence to support this. The *Semi-Weekly Messenger* wrote Murrieta was "as merciless as a hyena. He tied men to trees and left them to perish in the unfrequented forests; he raided towns and spared neither age nor sex; he raided Chinese mining camps and, on one occasion, cut the throats of eleven Chinamen in a camp near Sutler's Creek."

We know very little about Joaquin Murrieta other than he came to California, from old Sonora, Mexico, sometime in 1850 to try his luck in the goldfields. It is likely his wife, Rosa, several of her brothers, and his brother Carlos came with him.

The clan staked a claim near Hangtown. It is speculated they lost their property due to the Foreign Claim Tax (a penalty imposed on non-white miners to keep them out of California). In 1851, Joaquin Murrieta joined his brother-in-law, Claudio Feliz's gang. That was his introduction to outlawry. No matter how you slice it, these guys were no angels. They robbed and murdered lone travelers. Claudio's band terrorized the minefields for two years until they were recognized as they tried to rob the John Kottinger Rancho near Pleasanton. Shortly after that, they changed their MO and robbed a native Californian rather than their usual prey of Chinese immigrants. Vigilantes tracked the gang down, and Claudio was killed fighting off his pursuers.

Joaquin Murrieta assumed leadership of the band after the death of Claudio Feliz. Manuel Garcia, better known as Three Finger Jack, served as his headman. Together they began a six-month reign of terror in Calaveras County, beginning in 1853.

Governor John Bigler organized the California Rangers on May 11, 1853. They were an elite group led by former Texas Ranger Harry Love and charged with taking down Murrieta's band, known as *The Five Joaquin's*. The group consisted of Joaquin Murrieta, Joaquin Botellier, Joaquin Carillo, Joaquin Ocomorenia, Joaquin Valenzuela, and Three Finger Jack.

"Three Finger Jack was a monster of vice and maniacal cruelty." The *Yale Expositor* said, "He seemed to take a special delight in murdering Chinese. On one occasion, he rounded up six Chinamen on the road, tied their ques together, and cut their throats one at a time—laughing at the terrified yells of the living as the dying men struggled in their blood."

During their short career, the Five Joaquins rustled 100 horses, stole over $100,000 in gold, and killed between 19 and 22 men (most of them Chinese).

Their operations centered around the San Joaquin Valley. It became a common occurrence for them to rob the stage around Bakersfield. No road was safe. "The solitary horseman rounding a clump of chaparral was quite likely to hear the sing of a Riata through the air and feel the rope settling around his shoulders with a jerk that dragged him from the saddle. The Riata and the Bowie knife were the main weapons of Murrieta's men. "Many of Murrieta's victims were dragged from the saddle and had their throats slit."

Harry Love, and the California Rangers, received a break in July of 1853 when they captured Jesus Feliz, a brother of Claudio Feliz. He ratted Murrieta out and gave the Rangers the location of his hideout.

Love's posse came across Murrieta's band near Cantua Creek on the morning of July 25, 1853. While scouring the countryside for the band, they came upon a party of Mexicans eating breakfast. Love asked what they were doing, and the Mexicans said they were on their way to Los Angeles.

The posse would likely have ridden on, but as one of the rangers who knew Murrieta by sight rode up, the Mexicans made a run for it. Three Finger Jack was shot and killed immediately, along with several other gang members. Joaquin jumped on a horse and fled for his life. He was shot in the wrist and fell off his horse. Murrieta dropped his gun and threw up his hands. The posse disregarded his attempt to surrender and filled Murrieta with lead.

After the posse killed Murrieta, Love had them chop off his head and Three Finger Jack's signature hand. Then, they preserved them in jars of whiskey and brought them back to Governor Bigler as proof they had earned their reward of $1,000. State legislators were so happy to end the band's reign of terror; they awarded the posse an additional $5,000 bonus the following year.

After they collected their reward, Harry Love and the California Rangers displayed the jar containing Murrieta's head around the Mariposa mining camps for $1.00 a peek. Murrieta's head eventually made its way to the back bar at the Golden Nugget Saloon and was later destroyed in the San Francisco earthquake in 1906.

Sam Bass – Texas Outlaw

The Texas cowboy turned outlaw, Sam Bass, had a short-lived career robbing stagecoaches and trains. After his capture by the Texas Rangers, Bass told them, "I am shot all to pieces."

Bass left his home in Denton County, Texas, in the spring of 1877 and headed toward San Antonio in search of adventure. Not long after he arrived there, he worked on a cattle crew run by Joel Collins. They spent six months driving a herd to Deadwood, Dakota Territory. After they sold the herd, Collins paid off the crew, but instead of returning to San Antonio to pay off his investors, Collins went on a drunken bender and gambled away all the money.

Collins decided it was time for a change when he realized what he'd done. So, he gathered Bass and other members of the cattle crew and began robbing stagecoaches throughout the Black Hills. They robbed seven stagecoaches but got very little money for their effort.

    Sam Bass, Joel Collins, Jack Davis, Jim Berry, Bill Heffridge, and John Underwood picked up stakes and drifted to Ogallala, Nebraska, that fall.

    The gang conducted its first train robbery on September 20, 1877.

    A few minutes before the train's arrival, two masked men entered the office of John Barnhart, station agent at Big Springs, Nebraska. The robbers ordered him to destroy his telegraph equipment or take a bullet in the brain. Barnhart complied with their request.

    As the train approached the station, Bass ordered the agent to hang out the "red light," a signal to the train that they needed to stop for a mail pickup.

    The robbers dragged Barnhart to the express car and made him knock at the door. The *St. Louis Globe-Democrat* reported, "Miller, the express messenger, having no suspicion that any other person except Barnhardt was outside, opened the door a little way. When three of the robbers caught the door and, throwing it wide open, presented their revolvers at the messenger." Three robbers jumped into the car with guns drawn and began rooting through the contents. The take was $60,000 in freshly minted gold coins from the San Francisco Mint. There was another large safe, but they let it alone because Miller convinced the robbers he didn't know the combination.

After they had robbed the express car, the outlaws held up the passengers and got another $1500 in cash and two gold watches.

Before they could finish, the robbers heard the whistle from an approaching train. At the sound of it, they made their getaway.

Early the next day, two posses were hot on their trail. Sheriff McCarty of Sidney led one. Sheriff Bedley of North Platte led the other. About ten miles east of Big Springs, they discovered a rifle, a pistol, and a coin box, but the trail vanished as quickly as it appeared.

The robbery made front-page news all over the country. Passenger Andrew Riley enjoyed his fifteen minutes of fame after nearly being shot down by Bass's gang. Unaware a robbery was taking place, Riley stepped onto the platform. When he didn't stop at the first command issued by the bandits, they fired at him. One of the bullets grazed his forehead. Fortunately for Riley, he escaped with his life but lost $27 and his gold watch. *The New York Times* speculated the robbery must have been conducted by the James Boys or John Jarrett, noted outlaws known to be in the area at the time.

After the robbery, the outlaws met under a tree outside Big Springs to divide their loot, then split off into pairs to make their getaway. Each man rode away with $10,000 in gold and his share of the booty they took from the passengers.

Sam Bass and Jack Davis disguised themselves as farmers and made their getaway in a wagon. Davis escaped to South America. Sam Bass returned to his home turf in Denton County, Texas.

Shortly after pulling the train robbery, Joel Collins and Bill Heffridge rode into Buffalo Station, Kansas. The two men aroused the station agent's suspicions, and he ran to notify a company of ten soldiers camped outside of town. The soldiers quickly caught up with the robbers and ordered them to stop. The outlaws paused as they decided what to do, then pulled their guns, and began to fire on the soldiers. Outgunned, five to one, they were killed. The soldiers discovered the two men's share of the booty, $20,000 in gold coins, tied up in the legs of a pair of overalls.

Jim Berry made it home to Mexico, Missouri, but came under suspicion when he deposited a large sum of gold coins in the local bank. The sheriff rounded up a posse and tracked Berry to the woods behind his home. Berry was shot in the leg and died several days later from gangrene poisoning. Most of his $10,000 take was recovered. His partner in crime, "Old Dad," escaped with his share of the money and was never heard from again.

In early 1878, Sam Bass found himself short of cash and formed a new gang. Their first job was the Houston and Texas Railway at Allen Station on February 22, 1878.

After that, they robbed the station at Eagle Ford on March 18. The *Dallas Herald Weekly* told readers, "four masked men armed with Winchester rifles and navy sixes" approached the train depot.

One outlaw kept station agent J. Hixcox undercover. The other three marched the engineer and fireman to the express car.

When the messenger refused to open the door, one of the robbers grabbed a stick and beat on the door. The frightened express man let the robbers in and opened the safe. The robbers rifled it, then snatched all the registered mail from the bags.

After they finished, the outlaws backed away with their pistols drawn to cover their getaway. Texas Express agent Mr. Hargis estimated their take at fifty dollars. The mail agent said they likely got very little money from the registered mail. He wasn't aware of too much cash in the packages that day.

The station agent at Eagle Ford described the outlaw leader (Sam Bass). "He was a small man, rather wiry in his movements, with dark close-cut hair. He had the air of a border dandy."

The gang's next robbery was the express train at Mesquite on April 10, 1878. They rode up to the station and captured agent Jake Zurn. When the train chugged into the station at about 11 p.m., they grabbed engineer J. Barron and took him prisoner. Things went bad fast. Several members of the train crew opened fire on the outlaws. If that wasn't bad enough, a convict trained pulled up alongside the train Bass was robbing. When the guards discovered the train robbery, they opened fire on the outlaws. Unfortunately, the guards soon ran low on bullets and stopped firing because they feared their prisoners would attempt to overpower them if they sensed an opportunity to escape.

As the fighting slowed, the gang doused the express car with coal oil and threatened to fire it unless the expressmen opened the door. They threw the door open. The robbers grabbed what they could but made off with less than $200. The expressmen had hidden the bulk of the valuables during the fight.

The take from all three robberies was estimated to be slightly less than $3,000.

Less than a month later, the gang was looking for a big score to give them enough money to make a new start in Mexico. At about the same time, the Texas Rangers hatched a plan to catch Sam Bass. They approached Jim Murphy, a former associate of Bass, and offered him a "get out of jail free" card to help them capture Bass. Major John B. Jones had Murphy released on bail, then spread a story that he jumped bond. That allowed Murphy to rejoin the Bass gang.

Early in June, Bass heard rumors Murphy was a spy. The gang threatened to kill him. As soon as he realized his life was on the line, Jim Murphy laid his cards on the table. He said he agreed to rat Bass out to the Texas Rangers, but only to get out of the joint. He never meant to go through with the plan. The robbers let him live but kept a close watch on him after that—just in case.

On June 15, the gang left Denton County and headed for Austin, Texas. The first night out, they stopped in Rockwall and cased the banks. It looked like slim pickings there, so they moved on.

Leaving Rockwall, they traveled along the route of the Central Railway to Ennis Station. Murphy and Bass rode into town, grabbed dinner at the hotel, and spent scouted the bank. Finally, they decided it was too dangerous.

The gang's next stop was Waco. Jackson and Murphy rode into town to check out the banks. Jackson thought the State Savings Bank appeared to be an easy mark, but Murphy argued it was too dangerous. Later that night, Bass and Murphy rode back into Waco and grabbed a drink at the Ranch Saloon while they cased the bank. After giving it some thought, Bass decided it wasn't worth the risk.

The gang headed off to Benton the following day. Murphy got a note off to the Texas Rangers. He told Major Jones to set a trap at Round Rock. That night the gang set up camp two miles outside Round Rock on the International and Great Northern Railway.

They decided to rob the bank at Round Rock the next morning. The plan was for Bass and Barnes to go into the bank. First, Barnes would ask the cashier to change a bill. As he did that, Bass would put a pistol to the cashier's head and order him to throw up his hands. Then, Barnes would jump the counter and scoop the money into his saddlebags. Jackson and Murphy would guard the door to prevent people from coming in.

On June 19, Bass, Jackson, and Barnes rode into town to case the bank. Murphy went to May's store to get a bushel of corn for the horses.

The gang crossed the street and headed towards Koppel's store. Henry Koppel, the proprietor, was sitting outside the store as the gang walked in. Inside, the clerk, Jude, showed Bass several different brands of chew.

What should have been a peaceful exploratory trip turned into the massacre on Main Street. As they walked towards the store, the boys caught the eye of Deputy Sheriff Grimes. Grimes thought he saw a gun under Bass's coat, and carrying guns was against the law in Round Rock.

Grimes followed the gang into the store and told Bass, "I believe you have a pistol."

"Yes, of course, I have a pistol," replied Bass as he grabbed his gun and shot the deputy. Grimes staggered out the door and fell dead in the street.

That started a chain reaction that led to the undoing of Sam Bass.

Ranger Dick Ware raced out of the barbershop when the gunfire broke out. He found himself face-to-face with three of the outlaws. A stream of bullets plowed into the hitching post just inches from his face. The Ranger dropped to the ground and pulled his pistols.

Major Jones was in the telegraph office. At the sound of gunfire, he bounded into the street wielding a Colt double-action revolver and began to fire. Several townspeople had armed themselves and joined the fray by that time.

Things were getting too hot for the outlaws.

Barnes took a bullet and died on the spot. Bass was shot several times and struggled to get on his horse. Jackson jumped off his horse and held the Rangers at bay while he helped Bass climb onto his horse.

Sergeant Nevill and the Rangers discovered Bass the next morning. Texas Ranger John Gillett said, "We came upon a man lying under a large oak tree. Seeing we were armed as we advanced upon him, he called out to us not to shoot, saying he was Sam Bass."

Bass had taken two bullets—one in his right hand. The other was "pronounced fatal," said a story in the *Public Ledger*, published on July 26, 1878. The bullet "entered to the left of the spine, the ball tearing through the vitals and coming out the front aspect of the abdomen."

Bass died three days later from his wounds, but before dying, he told the Texas Rangers, "I am Sam Bass; I am shot all to hell, and it's no use to deny it."

He was 27 years old.

Jesse James and the James-Younger Gang

J**esse and Frank James are perhaps** the best-known bandits of the old west. During the Civil War, they fought with Confederate raiders William Quantrill and "Bloody Bill" Anderson. In October 1864, Frank traveled to Kentucky with Quantrill, while Jesse traveled to Texas with Archie Clement.

After the war, they returned to what remained of their home in Clay County, Missouri, and became outlaws shortly after that.

The James-Younger Gang committed their first bank robbery at Liberty, Missouri, on February 13, 1866. "A dozen desperadoes armed to the teeth and superbly mounted swooped down on the city." They overpowered the cashiers at the Clay County Savings Bank and forced them to stash over $72,000 into their saddlebags. While it's unlikely Jesse was involved in this robbery (he was still recovering from a severe chest wound he received at the war's end), Frank James, Cole Younger, and Archie Clement are said to have participated.

Just after noon on December 7, 1869, Frank and Jesse James robbed the Daviess County Savings Association in Gallatin, Missouri. Two horsemen rode up to the door of the Daviess County Savings Bank. One of them jumped off his horse and went into the bank. He ordered the cashier, John W. Sheets, to put all the money in a bag. The robber put a bullet in Sheet's brain and another in his heart. One of the riders slipped off his horse during their escape, got his foot caught in his stirrup, and was dragged for nearly fifty feet. The other rider came back to help him amidst a flurry of gunfire. The two men made good their escape with about $700.

Speculation had it Jesse mistook Sheets for Samuel Cox, the leader of the troops who killed "Bloody Bill" Anderson towards the end of the civil war. But it's more likely he got caught up in the heat of the moment and shot Sheets dead just because he could.

Six men rode up to the Ocobock Brothers Bank in Corydon, Iowa, on June 13, 1871. Three men entered the bank. Three men stood watch outside. The robbers inside the bank bound cashier Ted Wock, hand and foot and made off with nearly $9,000 in cash, gold, and stamps. As they rode out of town, the boys paused at a political rally where Henry Clay Dean was speaking. The bandits took a few moments to brag about the robbery and rode off, leaving the townspeople bewildered.

The Pinkerton Detective Agency said the James Gang switched tactics after the Corydon bank robbery and started robbing stagecoaches. They made a good job of it—working southern Missouri and Arkansas, particularly around Hot Springs.

The James Gang pulled their first train robbery at Adair, Iowa, on July 21, 1873. Nine men, including Jesse and Frank James, Cole, Jim, Bob, John Younger, Clell Miller, Bill Chadwell, and Charlie Pitts, derailed a section of track outside the Adair Depot just after 8:30 p.m. The gang expected the train to stop. But, instead, the engine and two baggage cars were thrown from the track when engineer John Rafferty slammed on the air brakes. Rafferty was crushed and killed by the engine. Fireman Dennis Foley was seriously injured.

Four robbers entered the express car and ordered the agent, John Burgess, to open the safe. The gang was disappointed when they discovered the safe contained only $2,000, so they robbed the passengers. While the men inside the passenger cars collected cash and jewelry from the passengers, the men outside fired their guns into the air to scare them.

As soon as they finished robbing the passengers, the robbers jumped on their horses and made a clean getaway.

The James Gang's next target was the Iron Mountain Railroad at Gad's Hill, Missouri. *The Salt Lake Herald* said the boys "took possession of the station, switched a train on the side track, and at their leisure…stripped the passengers of their surplus wealth and robbed the express car of $11,500."

The gang signaled the train to stop and started a small brush fire to ensure they would catch the train crew's attention. Five masked, heavily armed robbers hopped on the train as it slowed down. Engineer William Wetton and Conductor C. A. Alford were taken prisoner, along with the rest of the crew. One man rode amongst the cars firing his guns into the air to keep the passengers inside cowed. After they broke into the safe, the robbers took what they could from the passengers.

Jesse James handed engineer William Wetton a note for the press as they left. It read:

The most daring robbery on record

The Southbound train on the Iron Mountain railroad was boarded here this evening by five heavily armed men and robbed of _____ dollars. The robbers arrived at the station a few minutes before the arrival of the train and arrested the agent and put him under a guard, and then threw the train on the switch.

The robbers are all large men, none of them under six feet tall. They were all masked and started in a southerly direction after they had robbed the express. They were all mounted on fine-blooded horses. There's a hell of an excitement in this part of the country.

The Northfield Minnesota bank raid on September 7, 1876, was the farthest the James-Younger Gang had ever traveled from their home base in Missouri.

The *Salt Lake Herald* said, "on the afternoon of the 7, the desperadoes dashed into the town, shooting their revolvers and halting in front of the Northfield bank. The citizens on the street realized what was going on and opened fire on the robbers. Chadwell got shot off his horse...and, in just a few minutes...Clell Miller was also killed...Jim Younger had a bullet in his mouth, and Frank James one through his left leg."

Here's the way it went down. Three robbers entered the bank; the rest remained outside to keep watch. Cashier Haywood refused to open the safe. Bob Younger shot Teller Bunker in the shoulder as he attempted to escape through the front door. One robber shot and killed Haywood, saying it was "a warning to those bank cashiers to open up when we ask them."

Once the shooting inside the bank started, the gunfire outside picked up. The townspeople began an intense fire from behind doors and windows. "Two of [the robbers] fell dead from their saddles. A third was so sorely wounded that he nearly fell and was forced to beg his companions not to desert him. One of them got on the horse with him and held him during the retreat."

Clell Miller and Bill Chadwell died at Northfield. The posse killed Charlie Pitts during the pursuit.

The posse caught up with the gang as they crossed Lake Hanska Slough. Sheriff Gilpin ordered the robbers to halt. They refused and retreated to the Watonwan River amidst heavy gunfire. The posse chased them into the river and the palm brush on the south side of the river.

One robber threw up his hands and surrendered. He led the sheriff to where the rest of the gang was holed up. The *Mower County Transcript* reported, "Cole Younger and his brother were seen to fall and were heard groaning, and the other brother, wounded at Northfield, stepped out of the brush saying, 'Don't fire anymore, we are all shot to pieces.' Cole Younger and his brother were found lying on the ground, badly wounded."

Jesse and Frank James headed off in the opposite direction and made good on their escape.

It was the end of the James-Younger Gang. Jesse and Frank would later operate as the James Gang, but nothing they did after this would be as spectacular as the great Northfield, Minnesota raid or their earlier robberies.

Jesse James was shot and killed in his home on April 5, 1882. Not long after that, Frank James began negotiations with Missouri Governor Crittenden to surrender. Frank asked for clemency, but Crittenden made no promises other than to ensure Frank would receive a fair trial. Frank surrendered his gun belt and gun to the governor at the Capitol in Jefferson City.

After several weeks in prison, Frank was acquitted of all charges against him and released. Unlike Cole Younger and his brothers, Frank James never served any time in the penitentiary.

Bob Ford – "The Dirty Little Coward" Who Shot Jesse James

"There was never a more cowardly and unnecessary murder committed in all America than this murder of Jesse James. It was done for money."
**Evening Bulletin,
Maysville, Kansas
May 4, 1882**

Bob Ford is one of the old west's most interesting and least understood characters. Ford was an outlaw wannabe who teamed up with Jesse James sometime in 1881. There's no evidence to show Bob participated in any of the robberies committed by the James Gang. Charley Ford rode with Jesse James and participated in the Blue Cut train robbery near Glendale, Missouri.

The original James Gang had dwindled to just Jesse by the end of 1881. Most of the Younger brothers were shot up or imprisoned after the failed Northfield bank raid in 1876. Several members left the gang in 1880, fearing arrest.

Frank James moved to Lynchburg, Virginia, figuring it was a good time to go straight.

Jesse moved his family to St. Joseph, Missouri, in November 1881. Like Frank, he planned to give up the outlaw life and settle on a farm somewhere in Nebraska. But first, he needed one last score to retire comfortably. That's where the Fords came in. Jesse recruited them to help pull off his last job, robbing the Platte City Bank. The week before the robbery, the Fords moved in with Jesse and his family, masquerading as his cousins, Bob and Charley Johnson.

Unknown to Jesse, Bob Ford had a run-in with the law several months before this. He'd been arrested for killing Wood Hite. Rather than go to jail, he cut a deal with Sheriff James Timberlake and Missouri Governor Thomas T. Crittenden, in which he offered to deliver Jesse James—dead or alive. An article in the *Mexico Weekly Ledger* (Mexico, MO) said Bob Ford's first meeting with Governor Crittenden occurred at the St. James Hotel in Kansas City, Kansas, on February 22, 1882. Ford agreed to capture or kill Jesse James. In return, he would receive half of the $10,000 reward offered for Jesse James by the railroads and the State of Missouri and a pardon for his part in the murder of Wood Hite.

Bob and Charley Ford weren't sure they'd get an opportunity to kill Jesse James. He never went anywhere without a gun, and drawing a weapon without him seeing it was impossible. On the morning of April 5, 1882, Charley and Jesse spent several hours in the stable currying the horses to get them ready for their raid on the Platte City Bank the next day.

It was a hot, humid morning. The kind that made a man drip sweat. When they returned to the house, Jesse looked at Bob and said, "It's an awfully hot day." After that, he pulled off his coat and tossed it on a chair. "I guess I'll take off my pistols for fear somebody will see them if I walk in the yard." Next, he unbuckled his gun belt, which contained two revolvers, a .45 caliber Smith and Wesson, and a Colt. He then picked up a dusting cloth and climbed up on a chair to straighten some pictures.

It was almost like Jesse was asking for someone to shoot him. Charley and Bob Ford seized the opportunity. They knew they wouldn't get another.

They grabbed their guns and quickly stepped between Jesse James and his weapons. The April 5, 1882 edition of the *Evening Bulletin* (Maysville, KS) says, "Robert was the quickest of the two. In one motion, he had a long weapon to level with the muzzle no more than four feet from the back of the outlaw's head…The ball entered the base of the skull and made its way out through the forehead over the left eye."

Mrs. James was in the kitchen when she heard the shot. She rushed into the other room and found Jesse lying on the floor. The Fords told her, "it was an accident," as they slipped out of the door. Zee James "tried to wash away the blood that was coursing over [Jesse's] face from the hole in his forehead, but it seemed to her 'that the blood would come faster than she could wash it away.'"

The Fords telegraphed Sheriff Timberlake and Governor Crittenden that Jesse was dead. They were ready to collect their reward. Then, they turned themselves into local law enforcement officials.

Meanwhile, a coroner's inquest was held. Jesse's wife identified the body and accused Bob and Charley Ford of murdering her husband. Mrs. Samuels, Jesse's mother, identified the body. When asked if that was her son, she replied, "It is. Would to God, it was not."

The Watchman and Southron reported, "Governor Crittenden asserts positively that the body is that of Jesse James and that his death was the result of an understanding between the authorities and Bob Ford." It was a high point for the governor. It fulfilled his campaign promise to rid the state of Jesse James and his outlaw band.

The paper went on to say, "The Ford boys claim to have no object in view save to obtain the reward offered by Governor Crittenden for Jesse James, dead or alive. They had recently had two interviews with the governor at the St. James Hotel in Kansas City. The governor was informed of their plan of action and approved it wholly.

"After the shooting, they promptly gave themselves up to authorities." Their trial was one of the swiftest ever in the Missouri court system. They were charged, pled guilty, sentenced to death, and pardoned—all in less than twenty-four hours. Things didn't go quite the way they expected, though. The governor reneged on his promise to give the Fords half the ten-thousand-dollar reward on Jesse's head. Instead, they received less than five hundred dollars.

Bob and Charlie reenacted the killing in side-shows and posed for pictures with gawkers and curio hunters for a while. Then, as that business slowed, the brothers moved on with their lives.

Charley Ford suffered from bouts of depression and bladder problems. He visited his parents' home in Kansas City in early May of 1884. The only relief he could get from the pain came from morphine, and he needed more and more of it to get by.

The St. Landry Democrat reported his mother heard a gunshot and "found Ford lying on his bed, breathing hard, while blood was oozing from his mouth and nostrils. The pistol, a large Colt five-shooter, was placed against his breast over the heart. It burned a large hole in his outer shirt."

Like his brother, Bob Ford's life had its ups and downs. He wandered the west and tried his hand at odd jobs, such as gambling and running saloons. Bob and a friend visited Cannon's Gambling House in Kansas City on Christmas Day, 1889. They played a game of faro. First, Bob said, a man began to talk crazy about how he had killed Jesse James. Then "my abuser drew a knife from his pocket, and held my head back by my hair, and was about to draw the knife across my throat when my friend warded off the blow." The only thing we know about the attacker is folks around the gambling house called him "Fats."

Bob Ford quarreled with Deputy Watt Kelly over a girl in June 1892. The *Sedalia Weekly Bazoo* said, "Kelly stepped into the dance hall. 'Bob,' he said, holding his weapon ready for action. Ford was standing with his back to Kelly scarcely five feet away. He turned, and as he saw who called him, his hand went for his six-shooter. But he had no chance on earth. The shotgun, heavily loaded with buckshot, did frightful work at so short a range. Ten whole charges struck full in Ford's neck, tearing away his windpipe and jugular."

Bob Ford, the killer of Jesse James, died the same way he took Jesse's life—he was shot in the back by an assassin.

Rise and Fall of the Dalton Gang

The Dalton Gang enjoyed a short-lived crime spree for about eighteen months, beginning in early 1890. The funny thing is, before turning outlaw, the three Dalton brothers—Grat, Bob, and Emmett served as lawmen.

Their oldest brother, Frank Dalton, a United States Marshal, was shot and killed while trailing horse thieves through Oklahoma Territory in 1887. Then, brothers Bob, Grat, and Emmett turned outlaws in early 1890 after they had trouble collecting their pay for some law enforcement work they were involved in.

The Dalton Gang pulled off a handful of train robberies between 1891 and 1892.

The first train they robbed was the Atlantic Express on February 6, 1891. The boys flagged the train down with a red lantern they grabbed from the station agent. As soon as the train stopped, two men wearing long black masks stepped onto the locomotive and covered the engineer with Colt revolvers.

They forced the fireman to grab his pick-ax and dragged him to the express car door. They ordered the agent to open the door. When he refused, they busted down the door. In the commotion, the robbers shot and killed fireman George Radliff. The agent jumped through the window and escaped into the brush. With him went any hope the Daltons had of getting at the money in the safe. Unfortunately, in their rush to rob the train, the gang forgot to bring dynamite.

Disgusted, they fired their guns into the air and rode away empty-handed.

The Dalton's next robbery occurred at Wharton Depot on the Cherokee Strip. Three men rode up to the station at about 9:30 p.m. to meet the Texas Fast Express. Bob Dalton ordered the station agent to signal the train to stop, and then the gang pulled black masks over their faces before they boarded the train. The plan was the same as their previous robbery. They dragged the fireman to the express car, pick-ax in hand, and forced him to break down the door.

The Dallas Morning News, on May 11, 1891, reported, "It was a cool and successful piece of work done by experts. No shots were fired during the robbery, and most passengers were unaware of what was happening. When a passenger thrust his head out of a window, he was promptly made to withdraw it."

The robbery at Red Rock Station occurred just before 10:00 p.m. on June 2, 1892. An article in the *Norman Transcript* said, "Six masked men got on board and compelled fireman Rogers at the muzzle of Winchesters to break open the door of the express car with his pick, enter the car and smash the safe with a sledgehammer."

Another group of bandits made their way through the train, gathering cash and valuables from the passengers. The robbers fired a volley through the windows of the passenger car as they rode away. The take from the express car was slightly less than $2000.

The Dallas Morning News reported, "One of the more daring train robberies on record took place last night at Adair, I. T. As the Missouri, Kansas, and Texas north-bound express train pulled into Adair station, the train was held up, and everything of value to be found was taken."

Nine gang members rode into Adair station that night. They took everything they could inside the station, tied up the station master, and waited patiently on the platform for the train to arrive. It was a classic Dalton hold-up. They dragged the fireman to the express car, pick-ax in hand. When expressman George Williams refused to open the door, the gang fired shots through the car windows and threatened to dynamite the car. Williams opened the door, and they soon had all the valuables from the safe.

The *Dallas Morning News* added, "After a hard fight in which Chief Detective Kinney, Indian Policeman Laflore and two doctors, passengers on the train, were seriously wounded. None of the passengers coming to their aid, and their revolvers being empty, they were forced to retreat into the train...A posse was hastily formed and returned to the scene of the robbery."

The take was estimated as high as $70,000 or $80,000.

Bob Dalton had this crazy idea.

He wanted to make the Dalton Gang more famous than Jesse James. The only problem was that he had to do something spectacular, something never tried before, something so bold, so daring the newspapers couldn't help but take notice.

Emmett thought he was nuts when he told him what he wanted to do. Rob two banks, in the same town, at the same time, in a city where everyone knew you. It didn't make sense. Emmett said he went along with the plan because "he was damned if he did, and damned if he didn't." Even if he stayed out of it, he was sure the law would hunt him down.

The best account of the daring robbery was published in the *Coffeyville Journal* shortly after the robbery occurred. "Between 9:30 and 10:00 on Wednesday morning, [the

Dalton Gang], armed to the teeth and apparently disguised, rode boldly into [Coffeyville]."

The boys hitched their horses in an alley and headed to the two banks. Grat Dalton, Bill Powers, and Dick Broadwell entered the C. M. Condon Bank; Bob and Emmett Dalton hurried into the First National Bank.

Grat disguised himself with a black mustache and side-whiskers. He ordered the clerk to hand over the cash "and be quick about it." When a robber told the cashier, C. M. Ball, to grab the money from the safe, he told them he couldn't. It was on a time lock, and no one could open it for another three minutes. By that time, gunfire had erupted outside the bank, and the robbers made a rush for the alley.

Bob Dalton disguised himself with a mustache and false goatee at the First National Bank. "They covered the teller and cashiers with their Winchesters...and directed [the cashier] to hand over all the money in the bank." Bob and Emmett hurried out the back door when they heard gunshots outside and opened fire. Townsmen Lucius Baldwin, George Cubine, and Charles Brown fell dead.

By this time, all five bandits were in the alley, attempting to make their way to their horses. "A dozen men with Winchesters and shotguns made a barricade of some wagons. The robbers had to run the gauntlet of three hundred feet with their backs to the Winchesters in the hands of men who knew how to use them." A murderous fire poured through the alley for three minutes. "Three of the robbers were dead, and the fourth helpless." Dick Broadwell made it to his horse but was discovered dead about a half-mile from town.

Emmett Dalton was the only member of the gang to survive. They carried him to Slosson's Drug Store and later to Dr. Wells' office. There was talk about lynching Emmett, but what probably saved his life more than anything was the doctor didn't give him a chance in hell of surviving.

Bystanders carried the bodies of the dead gang members to the sheriff's office and later placed them in four varnished black coffins, where they were displayed and photographed so everyone could see them. Some people touched the bodies to make the experience more real. "Whenever Grat Dalton's right arm was lifted, a little spurt of blood would jump from the round black hole in his throat."

The next day, the entire town watched the undertaker shoo flies away from the bodies and nail down the lids on the caskets. Then, finally, the coffins were planted two to a grave in Potter's Field.

The *Galveston Daily News* headline on October 6, 1892, read, "The Dalton Gang has been exterminated—wiped off the face of the earth."

The only survivor, Emmett Dalton, received a life sentence in the Kansas State Penitentiary at Lansing.

However, he was pardoned by Governor Ed Hoch in 1907 and lived until 1937. He later became a policeman and an actor. Towards the end of his life, Emmett wrote his story, *When the Daltons Rode*, published in 1931.

Black Bart – California's Gentleman Bandit, Stagecoach Robber, and PO8

B**lack Bart was a dapper-looking gentleman.** No one would ever have suspected him of being a stagecoach robber. If you met Bart on the street, you most likely would have taken him for a prosperous business person. He wore only the finest hand-tailored clothes, stayed in the best hotels, sported a gold pocket watch, and wore a large diamond ring on his finger.

Bart stood ramrod straight, 5 feet, 8 inches tall, with grey hair and a bushy mustache. And, when he robbed a stage, he was always on his best manners and asked the driver to "Please throw down the box."

Bart's first robbery occurred on Funk Hill, a mountain pass in Calaveras County, California, on July 26, 1875. John

Shine drove the stage that day. Bart appeared from out of nowhere. He wore a long, soiled duster; on his head, he wore a flour sack with holes cut in it for his eyes. He waved his shotgun as he talked. Bart asked the driver to "Please throw down the box."

John Shine looked around, not sure what to do. He could always make a run for it or grab his rifle. But, from the corner of his eyes, he caught a glimpse of six rifle barrels pointed at him from a group of nearby boulders.

Shine tossed down the box and drove away as commanded. However, he saw Bart begin to hammer away at the box with a hatchet as he left. When he got a little farther away, Shine stopped the coach and walked back to the robbery site. Upon further investigation, he discovered the broken, strongbox and realized the gun barrels he'd seen earlier were nothing more than sticks that had been positioned in the boulders to make it appear like a gang of cutthroats backed up Bart.

Black Bart's fourth robbery occurred four miles outside Fort Ross in Sonoma County, California, on August 3, 1877. He left a mysterious poem that gave him his name.

I've labored long and hard for bread
For honor and for riches
But on my corns, too long you've tread
You fine-haired Sons of Bitches

Black Bart, the PO8

Almost a year later, on July 25, 1878, Bart robbed another stage about a mile from Barry Creek Sawmill in Butte County, California. Investigators found another poem in the strongbox.

Here I lay me down to sleep
To wait the coming morrow
Perhaps success, perhaps defeat
And everlasting sorrow.
Let come what will. I'll try it on,
My condition can't be worse,
But if there's money in the box,
It's munny in my purse.
                    Black Bart, PO8

The press had a field day. They printed and reprinted the poems and spent endless days deciphering their meaning.

During his eight-year crime spree, Bart robbed twenty-eight stagecoaches, all of which belonged to Wells Fargo. He never fired a shot in any of the robberies. In fact, there is some question about whether his shotgun was loaded. Unlike Belle Starr, Jesse James, and the Younger Brothers, Bart never took a dime from a passenger. Bart said Wells

Fargo's gold was reward enough if they gave him their purse or possessions.

But that doesn't mean the stagecoach drivers didn't fire at him. Bart jumped in front of a stagecoach driven by George W. Hackett on July 13, 1882. Hackett grabbed his rifle and let loose a flurry of bullets. Bart ran like a chicken with his head cut off as he hurried towards the trees. One of the bullets grazed his head and left a mark he would carry for the rest of his life.

Bart's final robbery has been described many times, and there are as many versions of it as Carter has pills. However, this account seems to be the one most agreed-upon.

It occurred near the spot where he pulled his first job. Reason E. McConnell drove the stagecoach up Funk Hill that day. Just as he rounded the bend of Yaqui Gulch, a hooded stranger jumped in front of him, shotgun in hand.

Bart requested McConnell to "Please throw the box down." McConnell replied that he couldn't. The box was bolted to the floorboards of the coach.

Bart ordered the driver to get off the coach and put rocks under the wheels so the stagecoach wouldn't roll backward. Then he had McConnell unhitch the horses and told him to walk away. McConnell testified that as he walked away, he saw the bandit whack at the box with a hatchet.

A short while after he left, McConnell met up with Jimmy Rolleri, a passenger; he'd let off the stage earlier to do some hunting. They returned to the stagecoach and fired a barrage of bullets that sent Bart scurrying into the woods. Finally, McConnell and Rolleri hitched the horses up and headed back into town. Later, they escorted a team of Wells Fargo detectives to the robbery scene.

The detectives scoured the area and found a small valise. One of the items they discovered inside it eventually proved Bart's undoing. It was a linen handkerchief with the laundry mark FXO7.

Back at Wells Fargo headquarters, detective James Hume assigned Harry Morse to check with each of the 91 laundries in San Francisco. A week into the search Phineas Ferguson at Biggs California Laundry recognized the handkerchief. He directed Morse to Thomas C. Ware, who ran a local tobacco shop. Ware identified Bart as Charles Boles and gave the detective his home address. A few days later, Morse returned to ask a few more questions, and as the two men talked, Ferguson noticed Boles walking down the street and offered to introduce him.

Morse struck up a conversation with Bart and told him he was interested in mining. He invited Bart into his office at Wells Fargo, where they met Detective James Hume.

Bart played it cool at first. He didn't say anything about the robberies. But eventually, the detectives searched his room and found several handkerchiefs with laundry marks that matched the ones found at the robbery site. They also found a duster like the one worn by the robber. Next, they had Reason McConnell and another driver meet with Bart. Both men identified him.

With overwhelming evidence against him, Bart confessed and took the detectives to where he stashed the gold. At his trial, he pled guilty to one stagecoach robbery, for which he received a sentence of six years in San Quentin. However, Bart was a model prisoner and secured an early release for good behavior on January 21, 1888.

Just over a month later, Bart disappeared from the face of the earth, never to be heard from again.

Here's what we know about Black Bart.

Bart's real name was Charles E. Boles. He was born in England. His parents moved to the United States when he was two years old. Charles and his cousin Dave headed to California in 1849, hoping to strike it rich in the goldfields. They didn't have any luck and returned home the following year. Charles, his brother Robert, and Dave returned to California to try their luck again in 1852. Unfortunately, shortly after their arrival Dave and Robert took sick and died.

Charles threw in the towel and headed back east. He wound up in Illinois, where he married Mary Johnson in 1854. He farmed there until the civil war, then enlisted in the 116th Regiment of Illinois Infantry. He participated in several major campaigns, including Sherman's March on Atlanta.

After the war, Bart returned home to Mary and the kids in Illinois, but he soon grew restless and struck off for the goldfields in Montana. He staked a claim there with Henry Roberts near Deer Creek. Several gentlemen associated with Wells Fargo tried to buy their land after they set up their claim. When they wouldn't sell, the men shut off the water flow to their sluices, and Charles was forced to abandon his claim.

Several years later, Charles Boles turned to a life of crime, robbing only Wells Fargo Stagecoaches.

Charles never admitted he was Black Bart. The name he gave prison officials was Charles Bolton or T. Z. Spalding. His real name is known because he wrote numerous letters home to Mary in Illinois.

Investigators believe he chose Black Bart after a favorite character from a popular science fiction story written in 1871, The Case of Summerfield.

Belle Starr – Female Bandit of Indian Territory

Belle Starr was "a sure shot and murderess, who never forgot an injury nor forgave a foe." She said she never killed a man she didn't have to, adding, "Wouldn't you kill rather than to be killed?"

On February 3, 1846, Belle Starr was born in Carthage, Missouri. Her father was a Southern sympathizer, and her brother rode with Quantrill's Raiders. As a young girl, Belle is said to have carried messages for her brother and, at one time or another, met up with Jesse James and the Younger brothers.

Rumors persist about an affair with Cole Younger, but the chances that it happened are exceedingly slim. She did marry his cousin, Bruce Younger, in 1880, but that union lasted only a few weeks. In 1866, Belle married James Reed, another outlaw who rode with Quantrill during the Civil

War. In 1868, she gave birth to her first child, Rosie Lee (better known as Pearl). In 1870, Reed was on the run for killing the man who murdered his brother.

On November 19, 1873, Jim Reed and Belle Starr robbed a Creek Indian, Watt Greyson, of $30,000 in gold and paper currency. Belle said, "Mrs. Greyson began to cry as soon as she saw us, screaming loudly for help. I approached her bed, placed my revolver on her forehead, and said: 'One word more and I will blow your brains out.'"

When Watt refused to tell them where he hid the money, Belle tied his legs and fashioned a noose. "We hoisted him to the branch of an oak," she said, "he began to strangle and signed to us to take him down. Thereupon he showed us his hiding place."

Upon returning to Texas, Belle held up a stage with her husband, James Reed. They made off with $3,000 of the stage line's money and another $2150 they collected from the passengers. They were discovered later that day as they ate supper at an Inn and had to shoot their way out.

Jim Reed rode off with John Morris in August 1874. The two men stopped at a farmhouse for supper, and Morris somehow convinced Reed to leave his guns outside with the horses. Morris made an excuse to go outside while they were eating. He grabbed his Winchester from his saddle and shot Reed dead at the supper table.

The story is Morris did it to collect the reward money on Jim Reed's head. Because nobody in the area knew Reed, the officials dragged Belle out to the farmhouse to identify her husband. Belle didn't want Morris to get the reward, so when the sheriff lifted the sheet covering her husband's body, she shook her head and said it wasn't him. Belle Starr repeated, "John Morris shot the wrong man."

Belle buried Jim Reed in a pauper's field. No reward was ever paid out.

In 1877 Blue Duck, an outlaw said to be Belle's common-law husband, borrowed $2,000 and dropped it all on the gambling tables in Fort Dodge, Kansas. When he told Belle, she was furious. She wasn't having any of that. Belle strapped on her pistols and headed for Fort Dodge. She crept upstairs to the "gambling hell" and took $7,000 at gunpoint from a private poker game.

Not long after this, Belle found herself running low on money. So she prettied herself up and pretended to be a fashionable member of Texas society, attending church and Sunday school. Within a short time, she was wooed by a middle-aged bank cashier. She visited him one day when he was alone at the bank. When she was sure no one else was around, Belle whipped out her revolver and a bag and demanded he fill it with cash.

After he handed her the money, Belle warned the cashier to keep quiet until she made her getaway, or she'd fill him full of lead. Belle jumped on a horse she had waiting at a nearby livery stable and rode off into Indian Territory.

Belle married Sam Starr, a Cherokee half-breed, in 1880 and set up house in a backwoods area of Indian Territory. Unfortunately, they had a run-in with the law for stealing horses. In 1882, Belle and Sam were sentenced to a year in the Detroit House of Corrections by Hanging Judge Isaac C. Parker.

Belle was arrested again for horse theft in the midsummer of 1886. She was taken to Fort Smith and acquitted in September of the same year. An article published in *The Dallas Morning News* on June 7, 1886, described Belle as she awaited trial. "Belle attracts considerable attention where she goes, being a dashing horse-woman and exceedingly graceful in the saddle. She dresses plainly...is of medium size, well-formed, a dark brunette, with bright and intelligent black eyes."

The same article said, "When at home, her companions are her daughter, Pearl...her horse, and her two trusty revolvers, which she calls her *babies*."

In 1886, Sam Starr got caught in the crossfire while being chased and was shot in the head. Fortunately, it was only a scratch. He managed to grab a rifle and shoot his way out. On Belle's advice, he turned himself in. The trial was held on March 7, 1887. Sam argued with a posse member about who shot the horse he was riding, and the next thing you know, the argument erupted into a gunfight. Sam was shot and killed.

Two years later, on February 3, 1889, Belle was killed in an ambush as she rode home from a neighbor's house. She took four buckshot in the back, three in the head, and one in the neck. The blast knocked her off her horse. When she was down, the attacker came in for the kill and blasted her in the face and neck with turkey shot.

Edgar Watson was the main suspect. They had recently argued over some farm property he rented from Belle. He was arrested, tried, and released. However, he received fifteen years in prison for horse theft not long after that.

Tom "Black Jack" Ketchum

Tom Ketchum was the second Black Jack to terrorize the Arizona territory. The first was a fellow by the name of Worthington. Lawman Les Dowe said they were the "very image" of each other. Dowe said Ketchum was "an absolutely dead shot with rifle or revolver. His nerve was past all question."

Tom Ketchum hooked up with his first partner in crime, Tom Sanders while working for the Chiricahua Cattle Company in the Sulphur Spring Valley on the western slope of the Chiricahua Mountains. The pay was a hundred dollars a month, and to earn it, a man needed to be "as handy with a gun as with a rope or a branding iron."

Tom Sanders was a real badass. Tom and his brother Charlie got shot up by a posse in Montana. They were captured, handcuffed together, then escaped. Unfortunately, his brother, Charlie, took a bullet and was killed in the shootout. Tom had no way out except to cut off his dead brother's hand.

Ketchum and Sanders began their robbery streak around Sonora, Mexico, sometime in 1891. They moved from town-to-town, robbing stores and anyplace else that looked like it might score them a few bucks. That got the locals riled up, and they soon found themselves racing out of town with a dozen Rurales hot on their asses, chasing them high up into the mountains. The boys killed five of the Rurales in the fighting that day.

Not long after that, Ketchum formed an outlaw band with Billy Carver, Tom Sanders, Bronco Bill, and Ezra Lay. They called themselves the High-Five Gang and operated throughout Texas and New Mexico. They robbed their first train at Stein's Pass in northern Arizona. Unfortunately, that one went sour from the start. The gang intended to rob the Wells Fargo express car but instead cut off the mail car. The take was nowhere near what they expected.

They robbed another train in Stein's Pass in 1895. Soon after this, they formed the Black Jack Gang, adding Sam Ketchum (Tom's brother), Harry Longbow, Gus Cassidy, Ben Kilpatrick, Jimmy Low, and Harvey Logan.

In 1897, they robbed an express train headed to Helena, Montana, and netted a cool $100,000 in banknotes. The only problem was that the notes weren't signed, so the boys had to turn into forgers before spending their booty.

Bad luck seemed to dog Black Jack's gang. Harvey Logan was captured not long after the Helena robbery.

Tom Sanders disappeared after the second robbery at Stein's Pass. No one was sure whether he was killed or decided it was time to move on.

The gang's next job was a train robbery in Folsom, New Mexico. In no time at all, a posse was hot on their trail. The boys were resting in the Cimarron country when Ezra Lay got up to get some water. That's when all hell busted loose. Sheriff Farr's posse had worked behind the gang and opened fire from behind a clump of rocks and trees. Ezra Lay was the first outlaw to go down. He was shot in the back and lay there swearing and mad. The boys probably would have laughed at his predicament if it wasn't for all the lead flying over their heads. Sam Ketchum didn't fare much better. He took a bullet in the arm that led to his eventual undoing.

In the end, the posse got the worst of it. Sheriff Farr and all his men got shot up and killed. The lone survivor was a newspaper reporter who tagged along with the posse. The outlaws let him live, but only because he'd hidden away during the fighting and had been too scared to fire a shot at them.

After that fiasco, the gang split up into small groups to make their getaway. Sam Ketchum got himself captured and cashed in his chips in prison. Billy Carver, Ben Kilpatrick, Gus Cassidy, and Harry Longbow got together to rob a bank in Sonora. Unfortunately, some locals recognized several of the boys during a scouting trip into the town. Billy Carver was shot at least six times and killed. Ben Kilpatrick got shot in the head and was never right again. He turned into a "driveling lunatic" and spent the rest of his days wandering throughout Texas.

In 1899, Black Jack rushed off on a fool's errand. He got it into his head to rob a train all on his own in Roswell, New Mexico. He flagged the train down and forced the engineer to bring it to a complete stop. Then he had the engineer and fireman uncouple the express car and move it away from the train.

Things went downhill fast. Conductor Harrington, who'd been robbed twice before by Black Jack's gang, decided he'd had enough. He grabbed a sawed-off shotgun and snuck up behind Black Jack. As soon as he had a clear shot, Harrington let loose and fired a charge of buckshot into Black Jack's arm and side. Harrington didn't bother to check whether Black Jack was dead or alive. After he saw the bandit go down, he signaled the engineer to get a move on, and the train hightailed it out of there.

Black Jack made his way to his horse but couldn't stay on his mount. He fell off his horse and spent the night in the rocks by the side of the track. He managed to signal a passing train the next day and hitched a ride into Trinidad, New Mexico. After the doctor amputated his arm, the sheriff hauled him off to the hoosegow.

At his trial, Black Jack told Harrington, "You've done me up. They're going to hang me." There was no escaping it. New Mexico didn't look kindly upon train robbers. So Ketchum was sentenced to hang and locked away in the penitentiary at Santa Fe to await his fate.

The execution occurred at Clayton, Union County, New Mexico, on April 26, 1901. Like everything else in Black Jack's career, his hanging wound up a hot mess.

He was brave enough.

On the gallows, Black Jack stopped to offer some advice to aspiring robbers. "Never steal cattle or horses, but stick to banks and trains and, whenever anybody interferes, shoot to kill, and a lot of bother would be saved." Before the hangman finished him off, Ketchum got in one last jab. He told his executioners, "I'll be in hell before you start breakfast, boys. Let her rip!"

And, let her rip, they did.

One hundred fifty spectators crowded around as Sheriff Salom Garcia chopped the rope twice with his hatchet. Then, finally, the trap door on the gallows swung open. The crowd heard a nasty pop as Ketchum's head tore from his body. The doctor stitched the head back onto the body before laying him to rest in Clayton's Boot Hill cemetery.

An article published in the *Topeka State Journal* on April 26, 1901, said, "The rope broke, but the fall jerked his head off." The *San Francisco Chronicle,* dated April 27, 1901, was more graphic, saying, "When the body dropped through the trap, the half-inch rope severed the head as cleanly as if a knife had cut it. The body pitched forward, with blood spurting from the headless trunk. The head remained in the black sack and flew down into the pit...for a few seconds. The body was allowed to lie there, half doubled up on its right side, with the blood issuing in an intermittent pattern from the severed neck."

That's how Black Jack Ketchum met his end.

Doolin-Dalton Gang, AKA The Wild Bunch

The Doolin-Dalton Gang was formed from the remnants of the Dalton Gang after their failed raid on the Coffeyville, Kansas Bank in October of 1892. The gang consisted of Bill Dalton, Bill Doolin, George "Bitter Creek" Newcomb, William "Tulsa Jack" Blake, Charley Pierce, and a negro named Israel Carr. Bill Doolin was the acknowledged leader, but "the negro Carr was said to have killed more men than all the rest of the gang put together." He was one mean son-of-a-bitch. Over time, the gang included Dan "Dynamite Dick" Clifton, "Arkansas Tom" Jones, and several others.

Bill Dalton wasn't part of the original Dalton Gang. Before 1892, he led a respectable life in California, where he ranched and served two terms in the California legislature. However, after his brothers got wiped out in the Coffeyville Bank raid, Bill Dalton decided it was time to shake things up a bit. He robbed his first train outside of Los Angeles,

California, in 1891. Then, in 1892, he joined Bill Doolin's gang and began a short-lived reign of terror throughout Texas, Arkansas, Oklahoma, and Kansas.

Bill Doolin was something of an enigma in Oklahoma Territory. Several newspapers published stories that made him out to be a "Robin Hood" type character. For example, Jack Dodsworth, a spy sent to infiltrate the gang, recounted a story about a man they robbed. Doolin took $35 from him but asked the man what he intended to do with the money. After the man told his story, Doolin calculated it would cost him $24.50 to accomplish his goal. So Doolin gave him back $25.00 and told him the extra fifty cents was to get himself a good meal. Another newspaper article said Doolin appropriated $300 from a peddler but gave most of it back so the man could cover the cost of his goods and get back home comfortably.

The Cimarron train robbery occurred on June 10, 1893. "Four masked robbers held up the California Express on the Santa Fe road" west of the Cimarron. Two men jumped onto the engine, with guns drawn, and forced the engineer to go to the express car with a sledgehammer.

The messenger refused to open the door. The gang blew it open with dynamite when arguing and shooting couldn't convince him to open the door. They beat it out of there with close to $1,000 in cold, hard cash.

Sheriff Byrns and his posse rode out after the gang the following day. They were close on the gang's trail but could never quite catch up. Finally, several travelers spotted the band along the lane east of Brannon's. At 11 a.m., they had lunch at John Randolph's ranch. Randolph had no idea who they were. The boys told him they were chasing a horse thief who got away.

On September 1, 1893, Marshal Evett Dumas Nix led a posse of 27 marshals and Indian police to Ingalls, Oklahoma Territory. They had received a tip that the gang was holed up in a saloon owned by John Ransom.

At the first sign of trouble, "Bitter Creek" burst out of the saloon, firing his Winchester at deputies. He took a bullet in the thigh but kept moving to make his getaway. Meanwhile, deputies kept up a murderous fire on the saloon. Finally, the outlaws escaped through a side door of the saloon and took shelter in a stable until they could hightail it out of there.

"Arkansas Tom" Jones opened fire from his hotel room window and was eventually captured. "Bitter Creek" Newcomb, Dan "Dynamite Dick" Clifton, and Charley Pierce all took bullets but managed to get away.

The Doolin-Dalton gang next raised their angry heads in Longview, Texas, on May 23, 1894.

"At 3 p.m....two rough-looking men walked into the First National Bank at Longview, Texas. One had a rifle concealed under his coat," reported the *Abbeville Press and Banner*. One of the robbers, Jim Jones, handed a note to bank President Clemmens. "This will introduce you to Charles Spelemeyer," it read, "who wants some money and is going to have it."

As Jones handed the note to the bank President, he jammed his rifle into the man's throat. The other man with him jumped over the counter and grabbed roughly $2,000, stashing it in a cloth sack.

Two other robbers were shooting it up in the alley outside the bank. City Marshal Muckleroy and Deputy Marshal Will Stevens returned their fire. "Bullets flew thick and fast, and the bank men hastened around the corner with several shots flying after them."

George Buckingham, a townsman who joined the fracas, was shot and killed in the crossfire. Muckleroy took a ball in the abdomen. J. W. McQueen, a saloonkeeper, heard the shooting and ran out into the alley. He was shot and mortally wounded. Another citizen, Charles Leonard, was enjoying a stroll through the courthouse yard when he took a ball in his leg. It later had to be amputated.

The papers reported one of the robbers, Gene Bennett, was shot and killed. He wore high-heeled boots, spurs, a full cartridge belt and carried two double-action revolvers. The marshals found 300 rounds of ammo packed on the saddle of his horse.

Two hundred shots rang out in less than fifteen minutes. If the gang had an inkling of what was to come, the odds are ten times that many rounds would have been let loose in Longview that day.

Bill Dalton cashed in his chips at Gidding's Ranch near Elk, Indian Territory, in April 1894.

The Daily Ardmoreite, on June 9, 1894, devoted an entire page to his death. The headline screamed, "Bill Dalton died with his boots on, pistol in hand."

The way it came about, Houston Wallace, Bill Dalton's wife, and another woman went on a wild spending spree in town, shooting nearly $200 in a very short period. It set off an alarm, and they were detained and questioned. The local marshal decided to check it out. He raised a posse and headed to Houston Wallace's ranch, arriving about 8 a.m. The posse split up and began to reconnoiter the place. At first glance, things looked normal enough. There were just a few women and children playing in the yard.

They probably could have taken Bill Dalton alive, but a woman tending cattle in the yard spotted them and raced towards the house to warn Dalton. "He immediately jumped through the window in the rear of the house, thinking that was unguarded." But that turned out to be a big mistake. "There stood Lou [Loss] Hart, true game, and a dead shot." Hart hollered at Dalton to surrender as he ran towards the nearby woods. But, when Dalton reached for his pistol, Hart fired his.

When they searched Dalton's body, officials found $325 on his person. The marshals also found a Longview Bank money sack in the house. That settled the question of whether Bill Dalton was involved in that job.

Bill Tilghman captured Bill Doolin at a bathhouse in Eureka Springs on January 16, 1896. It was more of an accident than anything. Tilghman bumped into Doolin in the bathhouse, quickly overpowered him, and took him captive.

Bill Doolin later told the *Guthrie Daily Leader*, "I was looking for a crowd with guns. I expected to be found sooner or later – felt that I would be shot down like a dog – and intended to do my share of the shooting. Had I been sure of Tilghman when he came into the door, I would have shot him dead in a twinkle."

Fortunately for Doolin, Tilghman didn't feel the same way.

After his capture, Bill Doolin was jailed in Guthrie, Oklahoma Territory, and quickly escaped in a mass jailbreak of fourteen prisoners.

Unfortunately for Doolin, he didn't think things through. He went to stay with his wife at her home in Lawson, Oklahoma Territory, where she was the postmistress. A newspaper report said Doolin didn't bother to hide that he was there. He rode into town several times, and local law enforcement officials turned a blind eye to his presence.

But when Deputy Marshal Heck Thomas learned Doolin was in the area, Doolin's days became numbered. Doolin left the house around 2 a.m. on the morning of August 25th, 1896, armed with a Colt 45 caliber and a Winchester rifle.

He walked out of the door and straight into the waiting posse. "The outlaw heard the command 'HALT!'" wrote the *Arizona Republican*. "Then someone cried, 'Hold up your hands!' Doolin brought his Winchester to his shoulder and fired two volleys almost as soon as the words were spoken."

"Thomas discharged his rifle. Doolin stumbled and, as he fell forward, fired off his revolver." At the sound of gunfire, the entire posse opened fire.

When the marshals examined his body, they discovered he had taken 21 rounds of buckshot and a rifle shot that shattered his arm.

"Dynamite Dick" Clifton – The "Most Killed Outlaw in the American West"

Killing Dan "Dynamite Dick" Clifton was a popular pastime among western newspaper editors who were quicker to print a story than to run a fact check. As a result, *Wikipedia* calls him "the most killed outlaw in the American West." There's no denying it. Just about every western newspaper published between 1895 and 1897 carried the gory details of Dynamite Dick "biting the big one"—going out with guns blazing, Winchester balls tearing through his body, leaving nothing but a blood-drenched carcass laying in the desert.

But, no sooner would you read about his death than he was robbing another bank, another train, or getting all shot up again. If he were alive today, "Dynamite Dick" would be "Kenny" on *South Park* or a popular victim in dozens of video games.

Legend has it Clifton got the name "Dynamite Dick" because he got a kick out of boring holes in his cartridges and filling them with dynamite. When they exploded, it made a hell of a ruckus and took a deadly toll on anyone or anything that crossed its path.

"Dynamite Dick" joined the Doolin-Dalton gang, or Wild Bunch, shortly after the original Dalton Gang had been wiped out in the Coffeyville Bank raid.

One of the first jobs he pulled with the gang was the robbery of the Ford County bank in Spearville, Kansas, on November 1, 1892. Three men rode up to the bank at about 2 p.m. One stayed outside to watch the horses. The other two men walked into the bank, revolvers at the ready. They put a gun to cashier Baird's head, snatched up all the cash in sight, and walked out over $1700 richer. As they ran out of the bank and jumped on their horses, a group of citizens opened fire. Fifteen shots crashed around them; fortunately, no injuries occurred in the exchange.

The bandits headed out of town with a posse hot on their trail. A running fight broke out on the trail, but the bandits made good on their getaway after a few well-placed shots.

On June 10, 1893, the gang robbed the Santa Fe Southern Express west of Cimarron, Kansas.

The *Meade County Globe* reported, "Four masked robbers held up the California Express." The robbers set up a danger signal about a half-mile out of Cimarron. When the engineer stopped the train, two men, with revolvers drawn, jumped onto the train and forced the engineer to go with them to the express car. The express agent refused to open the door, so they blew it with dynamite. It's thought the boys made off with about $1,000 that time.

All hell busted loose in Southwest City, Missouri, in May 1894 when the Doolin-Dalton gang robbed the bank. Over 100 shots were fired on Main Street as the boys made their getaway. Many townspeople said it "sounded like war times."

Seven men rode up to the bank at about 3 p.m. that afternoon. "Two of them were stationed on the sidewalk, three entered the bank with a sack, and two others guarded the horses." Bill Doolin pulled a gun on cashier Snyder and the bank owner, Mr. Ault. Another robber covered the rest of the employees while the third crawled through the teller window and began scooping up all the money.

A pitched fight broke out as the outlaws made good their escape. Four townsmen were wounded. Bill Doolin took several rounds of buckshot in the left temple close to the hairline but kept riding. A local paper said, "a posse was made up and started in pursuit, but the robbers have a good lead and will probably get away."

Their take was $4,000.

The *San Francisco Call* proclaimed, "Slaughter Kid and Dynamite Dick Riddled by Flying Buckshot." That was on May 3, 1895. A newspaper article reported the "dead men were stretched out on two boards" at Spengle's undertaking house. But, of course, they got some of the details wrong. For example, they said "Dynamite Dick" was Charlie Pierce, not Dan Clifton.

"Dynamite Dick" had "thirty buckshot in him, mostly in the right shoulder and side, although he had fully six shot in his stomach and as many in one foot. One Winchester bullet struck "Bitter Creek" in the forehead and tore out his brains at the back of his head, and the other hit his hand as he was pulling the trigger."

There was only one problem with that story.

A little later, in May of the same year, "Dynamite Dick" and the Doolin-Dalton gang robbed the Rock Island Railroad at Dover. They got several thousand dollars from the express car and some additional booty from the passengers.

Deputy Marshal Chris Madsen and seven posse members hit the trail in hot pursuit. "Tulsa Jack" Blake was killed during the pursuit. The other gang members got away, but their escape was short-lived. By the end of 1896, most of the Doolin-Dalton gang was dead or in jail.

Bill Tilghman shot up Bill Raidler and put him in jail. Next, Loss Hart killed Bill Dalton outside his wife's house in an ambush. Then, finally, Charlie Pierce and "Bitter Creek" Newcomb got themselves shot full of holes by a couple of bounty hunters.

In 1896, Deputy F. M. Canton tracked "Dynamite Dick" down and put him behind bars. Two weeks later, on July 5th, 1896, Bill Doolin, "Dynamite Dick," and fourteen other prisoners busted out of the U. S. Prison at Guthrie, Oklahoma. They rushed one of the guards, seized two pistols and a Winchester, and forced the guards into the cages. Deputy Marshal Lightman and his posse rode off in hot pursuit.

On October 18, 1896, six masked riders led by "Dynamite Dick" rode into the small town of Carney, Oklahoma, with their guns blazing. Two desperadoes busted into B. Fout's store. They forced him and his son to hand over the contents of the safe—about $800. After robbing them, the outlaws rode the two men a few miles out of town and tied them to a tree. While the Fouts were being terrorized and ridden out of town, the other gang members ransacked the post office, hotel, and several smaller stores, searching for anything of value. The outlaws kept up a "horrible commotion" the entire time they were doing that, screaming and firing their guns into the air.

When the boys finished their fun, they rode out of town in three small groups.

Several months later, in December, "Dynamite Dick" used up another of his lives. Supposedly, a posse trailed him and another gang member, Ben Cravens, to a spot three miles east of Blackwell, Indian Territory. The posse came upon the two men a little after daybreak.

The *Barbour County Index* said the Outlaws planned to rob the Bank of Blackwell at about 9 a.m. Sheriff J. R. Cox received a tip the day before that "Dynamite Dick" and Ben Cravens were hiding out at the house of a man named Hostler. He "organized a posse of seven good men in Blackwell, all of whom were splendidly equipped with arms, ammunition, and nerve." The posse challenged the outlaws to stop. But, instead, they opened fire. "At the first round," fired by the posse, "Dynamite Dick fell before the bullet of a livery stable keeper named Lang…who used a .56 caliber Winchester rifle ball." Cravens was shot three times—once in the shoulder, another in the lung, and the third in the leg.

The headline in the *Wichita Daily Eagle* on December 5, 1896, proudly proclaimed, "Dynamite Dick Bites the Dust." However, the editor of the *Shiner Gazette* dressed the story up a little, saying, "bullets fell thick and hot on all sides for half an hour."

"Dynamite Dick" played out his final hand in 1897.

Even then, several stories circulated about how he met his maker. The most published said Deputy Marshal George Lawson and Hess Bussey tracked Clifton to a cabin west of Checotah, Indian Territory.

The posse hollered for "Dynamite Dick" to surrender. As they did, a woman and boy attempted to leave the cabin. The officers told them to set the place on fire, but they refused and hurried back in.

Moments later, "Dynamite Dick" burst through the door—with a six-shooter in both hands, blasting at the marshals. Seconds later, "Dynamite Dick" fell dead for real.

Another version of the story says the marshals tracked "Dynamite Dick" to a wooded area in Indian Territory. They soon discovered that a man answering "Dynamite Dick's" description had been in the neighborhood for several weeks peddling whisky. Post office inspector Houck and the two deputies waited in the woods near Blair Hill, seeking clues. After two weeks of waiting, they discovered the robbers had gone to Keokuk Falls to replenish their whisky supplies but were set to return shortly.

When he got back, "Dynamite Dick" fired his Winchester into the air to let the locals know he had returned. The hooch would soon be flowing freely. The marshals watched the drunken orgy all night from their perch in the woods.

The following day, they moved in on "Dynamite Dick." He led a horse in one hand and held a rifle in the other. When the marshals challenged him to surrender, he raised his Winchester, readying to fire. However, the marshals were too fast. Dynamite Dick took a bullet in his left arm, dropped his rifle, and ran into the woods.

The lawmen tracked him all day. Finally, they located him in the house with a woman and a boy. The deputies ordered him to drop his guns and come out, or they would fire the cabin. At that point, "Dynamite Dick" decided he'd rather go out in a blaze of glory. He opened the door, armed with a pistol and shotgun, and fired at the officers.

The *Houston Daily Post* wrote, "After about twenty shots had been exchanged, Dynamite Dick fell dead, riddled with bullets."

"Dynamite Dick" had died his last death. But, surprisingly, the stories this time were shorter and less spectacular than previous accounts of his death.

Butch Cassidy and the Sundance Kid, AKA The Hole in the Wall Gang, AKA The Wild Bunch

The Wild Bunch, or the Hole in the Wall Gang, was one of the last great outlaw gangs to terrorize the old west. Butch Cassidy organized the gang, and membership changed as often as the wind, depending upon the specialties needed to perform the job.

Butch's friend, Elzy Lay, was the first member recruited into the gang. Other members included Harry Longabaugh, the Sundance Kid; Harvey Logan, alias Kid Curry; Ben Kilpatrick; Tom and Bill McCarty; Tom "Black Jack" Ketchum; Sam Ketchum; Bill Carver; and several others.

They hid in the Hole in the Wall, a secret lair; lawmen dared not enter. "It is a spot where ten men can defy a thousand," said a story in the *Saint Paul Globe*, "and one man can elude a hundred for months."

"The only entrance and the only exit is the gorge through which the little stream rushes out again into the open lower country. Here, too, the walls rise abruptly, like the canyons in Colorado, and so narrow is the trail that not more than two horsemen may ride abreast." All along the way, there are hideaways where one outlaw, armed with a shotgun, can make short work of a lone lawman or hold off a posse for days.

The outlaws would emerge from the Hole in the Wall—rob a bank or train—and dash back into hiding before a posse could catch sight of them.

The Wild Bunch's first job was the San Miguel Valley Bank robbery at Telluride, Colorado, on June 24, 1889. Four armed men rode up to the bank at about 10 a.m. as cashier C. F. Painter was out making collections. Three men walked into the bank; one stayed outside to hold the horses. The three robbers covered the lone teller with their revolvers and compelled him to hand over all the cash.

The robbery went off without a hitch, and the outlaws rode out of town with their guns blazing. They made a clean getaway with nearly $22,000.

One of the gang's boldest robberies occurred when they snatched the P. V. Coal Company's payroll at Castle Gate, Utah, on April 21, 1897. Three gang members made off with nearly $7800 while almost 100 miners milled about on the street nearby.

The outlaws watched and waited as the train delivering the coal company's payroll pulled up to the platform. Cashier E. L. Carpenter walked across the tracks with T. W. Lewis, another employee.

As Carpenter and Lewis neared the Wasatch Store, a man walked up to Carpenter, shoved a six-gun in his face, and ordered him to "drop them sacks" and "hold up your hands." The second robber began to whirl his guns in his hands, firing into the air.

The man with the money hopped on his horse and rode off at full speed, as did the outlaw holding the horses. The man firing his gun managed to escape, but his getaway appeared dicey when his horse got loose and wandered down the street. He had to chase after it for nearly 300 feet before he could jump on and ride away.

Several months later, on June 28, 1897, an off-shoot of the Wild Bunch robbed the Butte County Bank at Belle Fourche, South Dakota. Four masked men entered the bank with revolvers drawn and ordered the employees and customers present to throw up their hands. Cashier Arthur Marble hesitated for a moment. The next thing he knew, a shot rang out, and a bullet tore off a large portion of his right ear. No one got in the robbers' way after that. They quickly grabbed what money they could get, then rushed out the door and rode away.

A posse caught up with the robbers a few miles outside of town. After a running fight, outlaw Thomas Day threw up his hands and surrendered. However, four more robbers got captured at the VVV Ranch in Crook County, Wyoming. George Currie, the two Roberts brothers, and Harvey Ray were captured.

By all accounts, the take from that robbery was a paltry $75 to $100—not worth the time they would spend in jail.

Butch Cassidy and the Wild Bunch netted a cool $46,000 when they robbed the Union Pacific Overland Flyer No. 1 near Wilcox, Wyoming. One robber hopped into the train's cab and forced the engineer to pull across the bridge and stop. And then, "just as the engine pulled off the bridge, there was a tremendous explosion that scattered the express car for a hundred feet in every direction."

Mail clerk George Bruce testified the robbers ordered him to open the door. The robbers began shooting into the car from both sides when he hesitated. The next thing he saw was a stick of dynamite sliding under the door. He slid the door open and beat it out of there as quickly as possible.

Inside the express car, messenger Ernest Woodcock was the last holdout. He refused to open the door, despite bullets flying all around him. Finally, the robbers blew the door and pulled Woodcock out. The robbers must have been upset. Woodcock said they piled twenty sticks of dynamite around the safe and ended up blowing everything to pieces—the express car, the safe, and all the booty they were after.

The robbery lasted a full two hours. Much of that time was spent gathering the money scattered everywhere after the explosion.

After the robbery, the robbers disappeared into the darkness. Their take was nearly $30,000. It was a job well done, except for the blowing the hell out of the express car—and the safe.

Just after noon on September 19, 1900, three masked men, with revolvers drawn, entered the front door of the First National Bank of Winnemucca, Nevada.

"Cashier Nixon made a move as if to draw a revolver, but the weapon of one of the outlaws was aimed at him, and he threw up his hands just in time to save his life." The robbers forced Nixon to open the safe from which they took three bags of gold coins containing $5,000 each.

After grabbing all the money in sight, the robbers marched the five men in the bank out the back door and into the alley, where they had three horses waiting to make their escape.

The entire robbery took less than five minutes.

Townspeople exchanged a few shots with the robbers as they rode out of town, but no one was hurt. Then, a posse of fifteen men rode out in hot pursuit. The second posse of twelve men from Golconda set out shortly afterward. They planned to box the robbers in, but it didn't happen.

The Wild Bunch had relays of horses waiting at several points along their escape route. The first relay was located seven miles outside of Winnemucca. The second relay was at the Silva Ranch, about thirty-five miles northeast of the robbery. That was the "secret sauce" that allowed Butch Cassidy to escape so easily. Fast, fresh horses gave him an edge over his pursuers. It was a simple innovation in the robbery game. One, it's hard to imagine no one had thought of or used before.

Shortly after 8:30 p.m. on August 29, 1900, the Wild Bunch robbed Union Pacific passenger train No. 3 near Tipton Station in Wyoming. A man crawled down from the tender with his revolver leveled and forced the engineer to stop the train.

Conductor Ed Kerrigan said he felt the train stop just outside of Tipton. He saw a small fire and a group of men moving toward the baggage car. The robbers forced him to uncouple the mail, express, and baggage cars so they could roll them down the tracks.

Engineer Henry Wallerstein, expressman Woodcock, Conductor Kerrigan, brakeman Fred Nash, and flagman William Kuhns were forced to line up a short distance from the train. One of the robbers stood guard over them with a Winchester.

Kerrigan said, "They blew the roof, sides, and end out of the baggage car and demolished the next car to it. Then, they put three charges on the safe before breaking it open. Then, after they got what they wanted, they went to their horses, which were tied nearby, and fled."

The robbery was a major fail. Railroad officials said the gang netted less than $100.

Deputy Marshal Joe Lefors of Cheyenne, Wyoming, determined "the Tipton holdup and the Wilcox affair were managed in the same manner, and the robbery executed in precisely the same way." There was no doubt in his mind; both robberies were the work of Butch Cassidy and the Wild Bunch.

By the end of 1900, the old west was fading away. Civilization extended from coast to coast. Changing technology was making the West less isolated and more connected. Telephones and telegraphs made it easier to spread the alarm after a robbery. The Pinkertons and railroads were determined to put the robbers out of business, so they arranged for a special train to quickly rush detectives to the robbery scene. It had a sleeping car for the detectives on board and mobile stables stocked with fast horses specially trained to help in the pursuit of outlaws. The Hole in the Wall and Robbers Roost were still impenetrable, but no one could say how long that would last.

Butch, Sundance, and Etta Place decided it was time to change scenery if they intended to stay alive. So, they traveled to Texas and New York before hopping a steamer to Argentina on February 21, 1901.

They landed at Buenos Ayres, took a steamer to Bahia Blanca, and traveled by mule from Rawson to Chubut. By all accounts, they settled into a comfortable life, ranching in the Cholila Valley for their first several years in Argentina.

After that, they slipped back to their old ways, robbing payroll trains and stage shipments. No one knows what made them pick up their guns again. Maybe their money ran out? Perhaps they missed the excitement?

Information on Butch and Sundance during this period is sketchy at best. They robbed payroll trains and sometimes acted as guards for payroll shipments. Sometimes they played both sides—guarding the payroll until an opportunity arose to steal it.

In 1906, the *New York Herald* reported Butch Cassidy, the Sundance Kid, and Kid Curry were robbing banks and trains in Argentina. A newspaper report said the boys robbed the Villa Mercedes Hotel in San Luis. One man covered the clerk; the other two grabbed the cash and valuables. When the manager walked in, they shot him dead.

The *New York Herald* continued, saying one of the robbers is "a pretty little woman, 26 years old, with a gracefully girlish figure, flashing eyes, regular features, brilliant white teeth, and a mess of wavy hair." She was presumed to be Mrs. Longabaugh. She held the horses during the Villa Mercedes robbery.

From the sound of things, Etta Place disappeared sometime in 1907. No one is sure what happened—maybe life in South America wasn't her cup of tea. Perhaps she died? No one is certain.

The accepted story is that Butch and Sundance died in a shootout with law enforcement authorities in San Vicente, Bolivia, on November 6, 1908.

The real story isn't as dramatic as in the movie *Butch Cassidy and the Sundance Kid*. The boys most likely never made that mad last dash out the door, as portrayed by Paul Newman and Robert Redford.

Here's the way it happened. Two masked Americans robbed a mining payroll near San Vicente, getting away with 15,000 Bolivian pesos. After dark, they went into town and spent the next few nights in a boarding house. The boarding house owner became suspicious of the two Americans, especially their mule, because it bore the brand of a nearby mine. He shared his suspicions with the local military.

On May 6, a group of law enforcement officials surrounded the boarding house and ordered Butch and Sundance to come out. When that didn't happen, a gunfight broke out. Some witnesses say they heard a man's scream, followed by two gunshots. When detectives entered the property the next morning, they found two-shot-up Americans with bullet holes in their heads. Speculation had it; one robber killed his partner, then took his life rather than surrender.

Of course, old-timers in Wyoming and Montana say Butch and Sundance didn't die that day in Bolivia. Instead, they returned to their old stomping grounds and lived well into the 1920s or 1930s.

A similar story is told about another member of the gang. Kid Curry was part of the gang that robbed the Denver and Rio Grande train near Parachute, Colorado, on June 8, 1904. The gang blew two safes and shot one employee before getting away. The *Havre Herald* reported the posse shot Kid Curry during their pursuit. "As soon as he fell, he was seen to shoot himself in the head."

The only problem was stories abound about Kid Curry robbing banks and trains as late as 1908. And, if that isn't confusing enough, the *New York Herald* placed him in South America with Butch and Sundance in 1906.

Another gang member, Elzy Lay, got killed in a fight with Mexican officers near Patro Migros on the Mexico-Texas border. Seven men died in that fight, including Lay, two of his outlaw companions, and four Mexican officers.

The Wild Bunch had taken its final ride.

Pearl Hart - "The Lady Bandit"

***C**osmopolitan Magazine,* **more, or less,** created the legend that was Pearl Hart in an article they published in October of 1899.

They said the lady bandit "directed the affair. The woman held a revolver in one hand, the muzzle of the weapon looking threateningly, now on one person and now on another. The woman was in a man's garment, and in the moonlight, her slender (read between the lines: sexy) figure and the masses of hair escaping from beneath the broad sombrero were plainly discernible."

It was a story that was too good to ignore.

Within a few days, papers from all over the country borrowed quotes from the article, telling readers about the brash, cigar-smoking, hard-drinking "lady bandit" who masterminded the daring daylight stage robbery.

Pearl told readers she came from a good home and had attended a private boarding school, but she hooked up with a fast-talking conman and gambler at the tender age of sixteen. "Marriage to me was but a name," she said. "We ran away one night and were married."

It didn't take Pearl long to figure out that her new husband, Frank Hart, wasn't exactly marriage material. He drank, gambled to excess, and frequently beat and abused her. They broke up and got back together at least three times.

The couple headed to Chicago in 1893. Pearl said they planned to fleece visitors to the Columbian Exposition. But, before that happened, she attended a performance of *Buffalo Bill's Wild West Show*. After that, Pearl became enamored with cowboys and the old west. Finally, after taking another drubbing from Frank Hart, Pearl decided enough was enough. She abandoned her husband, sent her son home to live with her mom in Ohio, and hopped on a train to Colorado and Arizona.

Pearl took a job cooking (some reports said she gave the men more comfort than food, but no proof exists that she prostituted herself) in a mining camp in the Pinal Mountains.

After a short spell cooking, Pearl hooked up with Joe Boot. They staked a claim in the Pinal Mountains, but the takings were slim.

In May 1899, Pearl said she received word her mother was dying. She grew desperate to get home to see her. Money was tight, so they hatched a plan to rob a stagecoach.

They rode out to a bend in the road that the stagecoach would have to pass. It seemed like the perfect spot, so they waited and listened for the stage.

They approached it at a slow trot as it came closer to them. Joe Boot pulled his Colt .45 and screamed at the driver to "throw up his hands."

Pearl pulled out her .38, got off her horse, and went to work collecting booty from the passengers. All the while, Joe remained on his horse and kept everyone covered.

Pearl couldn't understand "why men carry revolvers because they almost invariably give them up at the very time they were made to be used." She took two revolvers from the passengers that day.

The most frightened passenger carried the most money. Pearl snatched $390 out of his pockets. She told reporters the man was trembling so hard she had difficulty getting her hands in his pockets.

Pearl described the other fellow as a "dude" who parted his hair in the middle. He "tried to tell me how much he needed the money," she said. But his sob story didn't stop Pearl from rustling through his pockets. She took $36 from him. The last passenger was a Chinaman. He was plenty scared and trembling, but Pearl remarked he was easy to search because he was a little fellow close to her size. All he had on him was $5.00.

They decided not to take the driver's money. Instead, Pearl took his pistol. That proved a big mistake, but we will get to that in its own time.

When they were finished robbing the passengers, Pearl gave them "a charitable contribution of a dollar apiece and ordered them to move on."

Their getaway was a bungled mess. Pearl told a harrowing story of their escape. The duo traveled fast, and what they thought was far, but mostly, they rode around in circles. Eventually, they found a quiet space to bed down. "About three hours after laying down," she says, "we were awakened by yelling and shooting. We sprang up and grabbed our guns but found we were looking straight into the mouths of two gaping Winchesters in the hands of the sheriff's posse. Resistance was worse than useless, and we put up hands."

In most cases, that would have been the end of the story, but Pearl was a novelty. She was a pretty, young female stage robber, and the press played the story for every extra reader they could wring out of it.

Then, in October 1899, the *Cosmopolitan* story catapulted Pearl into the national limelight.

The magazine described Pearl as "a small woman, weighing less than a hundred pounds, with features of the most common type. Donning a set of man's clothes and taking the necessary revolvers, and securing a male companion, she appeared on the highway. The leveled revolvers quickly brought the coach and its occupants to a standstill."

A short time after the article's publication, Pearl and Ed Hogan made a daring escape from the Pima County Jail in Tucson, Arizona. He had been locked up for public drunkenness a few weeks before the escape, and Pearl somehow charmed him into helping.

Hogan snuck out of prison on the morning of October 12, 1899. Later that night, he crawled up on the balcony and cut a hole in the wall outside Pearl's cell. The next day, the San Francisco Call headline read, "Famous Woman Bandit and Stage Robber Once More at Liberty: Helped By a Man."

The couple made their way to Deming, New Mexico, but got captured a few weeks later. Again, Pearl fell victim to her fame. A detective in Deming recognized her from the pictures published in the *Cosmopolitan* pictorial. Authorities quickly arrested Pearl and sent her back to prison in Tucson.

Not long after her capture, Pearl stood trial for the stage robbery. She walked into the courtroom wearing a pretty dress and charmed the jury. She told them she didn't want to do it. It was all Joe Boot's idea. She just wanted to get enough money to visit her dying mother.

Whatever she said, the jury bought her story - hook, line, and sinker. The jury acquitted Pearl after less than an hour of deliberation.

Judge Fletcher Doan was outraged by the verdict. He quickly empaneled a new jury and tried Pearl for stealing the stagecoach driver's ten-dollar revolver. In the new trial, Pearl received a five-year sentence. Joe Boot received a thirty-year sentence to the Yuma Territorial Prison.

He escaped two years later and was never heard from again. Finally, Pearl received a pardon from Governor Alexander Brodie in 1902 on the condition that she immediately leave the Arizona Territory.

The prison superintendent told the *Herald Democrat*, "Pearl had been a model prisoner, complying well with the regulations of the penitentiary, and was therefore entitled to lenient consideration."

Rumors on the street had it Pearl was pregnant, and officials were anxious to get her out of Dodge before they had to explain how she got into that situation.

In 1903, Pearl attempted to cash in on her fame by acting in a play, "The Arizona Bandit," written by her sister. It failed miserably. A year later, Pearl was running a cigar store in Kansas City. After that, she faded into oblivion and was never heard from again.

Western Bad Men

Bat Masterson knew better than most of his contemporaries that most of what was written about the old West was little more than rattlesnake piss and bat guano. In 1910, a reporter for the *Salt Lake Tribune* approached him to do an interview. Masterson told the reporter, "If there's anything that makes me tired, it's these young fellows who insist on writing a lot of trash about events that happened twenty years before they began yelling for their living. If they'd tell the truth, it wouldn't be so bad, but they have to dress it up and tell the public that a peaceable man like me has twenty-seven notches on his gun. Don't you say anything about those notches, and I'll let you have a few unvarnished facts."

What followed was an amazing look at some big-name gunfighters, their physical prowess, and how they fired so fast.

He said, "nerve was the quality that marked the great gunfighters." One example he gave was Charlie Harrison. He was "the most brilliant performer with a pistol." He could "shoot faster and straighter than many of the great fighters." But, when the shit hit the fan, and it was time for the real thing, he couldn't muster up the nerve. Harrison got in a gunfight with Jim Levy, someone he should have easily bested, but "he missed him with all six shots at close range before Levy could reach for his weapon."

"Harrison was brave, but he had no nerve." He lay dead in the street while Jim Levy walked away.

Masterson admired Wild Bill. Bill "made the average heavyweight prizefighter look like fun. There wasn't a man in the west that could have touched him in a physical encounter." He was as good with his guns as he was with his fists. The same was true for Wyatt Earp. He could handle himself with or without a weapon.

Perhaps more telling is what Masterson suggested was the "secret sauce" that made the big-name gunfighters fast.

"We used to file the notch of the hammer till the trigger would pull 'sweet,' which is another way of saying that the blame gun would pretty near go off if you looked at it." But "the real gunfighters didn't file the notches off." Instead, they carried one gun in their hip-holster and another "swung under the armpit." It let them "draw on an adversary while he was waiting for the familiar motion toward the hip."

An article published in the *Seattle Post Intelligencer* on July 22, 1900, took things a step further. They said the gunfighters "all filed the sights from their guns and shot by instinct rather than by aim. Triggers were a superfluous piece of mechanism, and all were addicted to the process in a fight, technically known as fanning their guns. By this means, a man with a brace of Colt's six-shooters becomes, for the moment, an animated machine gun," or in the terms of another early reporter, "a walking *Gatling Gun.*"

Some gunfighters resorted to dirty, underhanded tricks. Before Billy the Kid challenged Joe Grant, he stacked the deck in his favor. Billy snatched Grant's gun and set it to an empty chamber. That bought him the precious few seconds he needed to draw down on his opponent. Some would call what Billy did cowardly, but in this case, it was just one more notch in his pistol.

Some western aficionados talk about Tom Horn being a gunfighter, but he never faced his victims in a fair fight. Instead, Tom Horn favored ambushing and back shooting his victims. Some folks say he placed very little value on human life, but one thing is certain, he never took any chances when it came to his life.

A few gunfighters were just that good. By all accounts, John Wesley Hardin was "lightning fast." His landlady said Hardin was "quick as a flash. He would have a gun in each hand clicking so fast that the clicks sounded like a rattle machine." The implication was he fanned his pistols to produce that "machine-gun-like" effect. Some stories say he wore a magic vest with pistol holders on either side. So, he likely practiced the old fake out—reaching for his hip-pocket pistol while drawing from his vest.

If a gunfighter expected to stay alive, practice was the name of the game. "The drop is what the gunfighter worked for and figured for from the moment he strapped on a pair of .44 caliber Colts until he was laid out with boots on," said the *Semi-Weekly Messenger*. "Careful adjusting of boots and holster, the free easy slide of the gun in and out, so that there was no possibility of a stick or hand when in the act of drawing, were manners of constant care and study, and long practice enable the gunfighter to 'pull his gun' and bring it on the object with action almost quicker than the eye."

Another certainty is that claimed and confirmed kills are totally different animals.

Wes Hardin took credit for forty-two kills in his autobiography. An accurate count is most likely under half that. Likewise, if you listen to stories about Doc Holliday, you'd think he left a trail of dead bodies everywhere he laid his hat. Not so. Doc's confirmed body count is two, not the dozens usually laid at his feet.

.

Billy the Kid – New Mexico Outlaw, Gunfighter, and Cattle Thief

Charles Siringo, in his *History of Billy the Kid,* portrayed Billy as a crazed psycho-killer who made his first kill at age twelve. Then, Siringo said, Billy snuck off to Fort Union, New Mexico, where he gambled with the black soldiers. A "black nigger" cheated him, and he shot the man dead. Not long after that, he stabbed a man three times in a saloon fight and ran out of the establishment with blood dripping from his right hand.

Siringo blamed it on Billy's violent temper. However, sheriff Pat Garrett, who would eventually track Billy down, and kill him, said just the opposite. Garrett said people often talked about the look in Billy's eye and his temper just before he killed, but *the Kid* wasn't like that. Instead, Garrett said, Billy ate "and laughed, drank and laughed, talked and laughed, fought and laughed and killed and laughed."

The only picture we have of Billy the Kid doesn't do him justice. He looks more like a mental defective with a lopsided face than someone often described as a lady's man. Billy stood five foot, eight inches tall, weighed about 140 pounds, and had a stringy muscular build. His hair was a sandy brownish-blond, and the one personality trait that stuck out about the Kid was his sense of humor.

In other circumstances, he might have been a politician or a business mogul, but he was a gunman in the old West and one of the best at his trade.

Very little is known about the Kid's early life. He may have been born in New York or Indiana, but there is no evidence to favor either state. His given name was William Henry McCarty, Jr., but he went by William H. Bonney in New Mexico.

Billy's first *documented kill* occurred sometime after he turned sixteen. Frank "Windy" Cahill, the blacksmith at Fort Grant, got a kick out of bullying and pushing Billy around. One day he pushed him a little too far and began to chase after him and swear at him. Finally, he knocked Billy to the ground and pummeled his face. Billy was no fool. He knew he couldn't outfight Cahill, so he pulled his gun and shot him dead. The coroner's inquest labeled the killing a homicide, and Billy hit the trail one step ahead of the law.

Billy reappeared in Lincoln County, New Mexico Territory, sometime in 1877. He changed his name to William H. Bonney and began working for the Coe-Saunders ranch. Unfortunately, that move placed him smack-dab in the center of the Lincoln County War.

The Lincoln County War started in the summer of 1876 but heated up in the spring of 1877. The Cattle King of New Mexico, John Chisum, ran 40,000 head of cattle that ranged over a 200-square mile area. The smaller ranchers accused Chisum of swallowing up their cattle and placing the Chisum brand on them. Chisum claimed just the opposite. He said the small ranchers cut cattle out of his herds and sold them at the army posts for a quick profit.

Alex McSween was a prominent Lincoln County lawyer and ally of John Chisum. He originally worked as a lawyer for Murphy and Dolan but later switched allegiances to work as an attorney for John Chisum. Murphy and Dolan later claimed McSween embezzled money from them.

Alex McSween convinced John Tunstall, a wealthy Englishman, that Lincoln County was ripe for the picking. Tunstall bought a ranch on the Rio Feliz and set up a store and bank in the town of Lincoln. In doing so, he allied himself with the Chisum faction.

Lawrence Murphy and James Dolan ran the Murphy-Dolan store just down the street from Tunstall's new store. They had enjoyed a monopoly on business in Lincoln since

Murphy started the company in 1869. Because of that, they could charge the local ranchers exorbitant prices for their goods. So, when Tunstall opened his store, he charged lower prices and began stealing business from the Murphy-Dolan store.

Things soon turned violent, with each side employing hired guns to get their way.

In February 1878, Deputy Sheriff William Morton and his posse began to round up horses owned by Tunstall and McSween. They came across Tunstall riding with his herd. Morton claimed Tunstall pulled his gun, so he shot him off his horse. But, Pat Garrett said, when Tunstall was laying on the ground, Tom Hill rode up to him, placed his shotgun to his head, and "scattered his brains over the ground."

Richard M. Brewer, Tunstall's ranch foreman, was sworn in as a special constable in Lincoln, and his posse, known as the Regulators, rode off searching for Tunstall's killers. They captured Morton and Baker on March 6 but reported them killed in an escape attempt on March 9. The Regulators later ambushed and killed Sheriff William Brady and his deputy, Fred Waite, on the main street of Lincoln.

Violence continued to rage throughout the spring and summer of 1878. Finally, New Mexico Governor Lew Wallace (a former Civil War general and the author of *Ben Hur*) offered an amnesty for any man involved in the Lincoln County War who wasn't currently under indictment.

Billy sent Wallace a letter offering to testify in return for a pardon. Governor Wallace and the Kid met in Lincoln in March 1879 to negotiate for Billy's testimony. The story is Billy met Wallace with a six-shooter in one hand and a Winchester 73 rifle in the other.

Under the terms of their deal, Billy was arrested for a short period. When he finished testifying, he was supposed to be set free. Unfortunately, the Governor reneged on his promise, and the Kid soon escaped. Billy's life remained uneventful for the next year and a half. He stole a few horses and rustled some cattle. During this period, the only standout event was a bit of gunplay with Joe Grant—a gunfighter wannabe. The story is Grant went on a wild bender at Hargrove's Saloon and grabbed a gun from one of Billy's compadres. Billy got a hold of the gun, set it to an empty chamber, then challenged Grant to a fight. When Grant pulled his weapon, it clicked on an empty cylinder, and Billy shot him dead.

As soon as Pat Garrett was elected sheriff of Lincoln County in November of 1880, he rounded up a posse and set out after Billy. The Kid was outgunned and quickly surrendered to Garrett. Billy was tried at Mesilla, New Mexico, in March 1881 and convicted of killing Sheriff William Brady. The court sentenced him to hang on May 13, 1881.

Billy was confined in the old Murphy-Dolan store in Lincoln while waiting to be hanged. On the evening of April 28, Billy overpowered Deputy J. W. Bell, on the stairs outside of the prison, snatched his gun, and shot him dead. Inside the jailhouse, he grabbed Pat Garrett's rifle from his office and waited for Deputy Marshal Robert Olinger. After killing Olinger, Billy stole a horse and galloped out of town.

On July 14, Garrett received word the Kid was holed up in the abandoned ruins of Fort Sumner, and he rode off to bring him in. According to Garrett's account of Billy's death, published in his book *The Authentic Life of Billy the Kid*, he went to the ranch of Peter Maxwell looking for the Kid.

Garrett was in Maxwell's bedroom questioning him on the Kid's whereabouts when Billy stumbled in with a six-shooter in one hand and a meat cleaver in the other. It was dark, and at first, Billy didn't realize anyone was in the room with Maxwell.

Maxwell whispered, "That's him!"

The Kid jumped back, "raised his pistol, a self-cocker, within a foot of my breast. Then, retreating rapidly across the room, he cried: 'Quien es?' 'Quien es?' All this occurred in a moment. Quickly as possible, I drew my revolver and fired, threw my body aside, and fired again. The second shot was useless; the Kid fell dead. He never spoke. A struggle or two, a little strangling sound as he gasped for breath, and the Kid was with his victims."

Luke Short – Frontier Scout, Gambler, and Gunfighter

"**Luke Short was a little fellow**, so to speak," wrote Bat Masterson. He was "about five feet six inches in height, and weighing in the neighborhood of one hundred and forty pounds." And he was nothing more than "a white Indian."

The *Omaha Daily Bee* said Short was a scout for General Crook's cavalry in 1876 and 1877 during his Black Hills campaign. He was chased by fifteen Sioux on one mission and single-handedly killed five of them while escaping. As the Indians chased him, "Short returned their fire and dropped the three foremost in quick succession with as many bullets." Two Indians raced after him, "deliberately checking his horse's pace, Short turned in his saddle and dropped the two Indians one after the other."

That was the beginning of his legend.

In 1878, he killed two noted horse thieves over a game of Spanish Monte. After they lost all their money to Short, the gamblers demanded Short give it back. When he refused, they pulled their guns. "Short was too quick for them," wrote the *Omaha Daily Bee*. Both men dropped to the ground—dead, without a chance to pull the trigger.

On Friday, February 21, 1881, Luke Short got into a gunfight at the Oriental Saloon in Tombstone, Arizona. Short was sitting lookout at the faro table when Charlie Storms burst in with a mean drunk on. Witnesses said Charlie was itching for a fight. He started out by abusing Lou Rickabaugh, the owner of the saloon. After Rickabaugh slipped out a side door to escape Storms' harassment, Storms turned his attention to Luke Short.

Bat Masterson, who was good friends with both men, was there that night. When Storms challenged Short, Masterson said, "I jumped between them and grabbed Storms, at the same time requesting Luke not to shoot." After that, Masterson walked Storms to the street and told him to sleep it off.

It should have ended there, but...

"I was just explaining to Luke," said Masterson, "that Storms was a very decent sort of man when, lo and behold! There he stood before us. Without saying a word, he took hold of Luke's arm and pulled him off the sidewalk where he had been standing, at the same time pulling his pistol, a

Colt's cut-off, 45 caliber, single-action, but like the Leadvillian, he was too slow, although he succeeded in getting his pistol out. Luke stuck the muzzle of his pistol against Storm's heart and pulled the trigger. The bullet tore the heart asunder, and as he was falling, Luke shot him again. Storms was dead when he hit the ground."

Short was arrested and later acquitted. The shooting was ruled self-defense.

In 1883, Short operated the Long Branch saloon in Dodge City. One of his rivals, W. H. Harris, convinced the city council to pass certain restrictions on gambling houses. Short's problem was that they only enforced the restrictions against the Long Branch, not against anyone else. It didn't take Short long to see how the wind was blowing. He closed the Long Branch and headed off to Kansas City.

If Harris thought he'd outfoxed Short, he soon discovered that wasn't the case. Within days of his arrival in Kansas City, newspapers reported Short was plotting his return to Dodge City. The *Wheeling Daily Intelligencer* (WV) reported Short was assembling a band of "eight men: a greater portion of them are said to be the most desperate characters in the west." The men in Short's party read like a laundry list of characters from the 1940s and 1950s B-westerns—Bat Masterson, Wyatt Earp, Bill Earp, Virgil Earp, Doc Holliday, Curly Bill, Shotgun Collins, and Charlie Bassett.

Short and his crew reopened the Long Branch within three weeks of leaving Dodge City. This time, business flourished, and no one dared to challenge him. After that, Luke Short ran Dodge City from the barrel of a Winchester. He was the victor of the "so-called" Dodge City War.

Luke Short shot and killed Jim Courtwright outside the White Elephant saloon a few minutes past 8 p.m. on February 10, 1887.

Officer "Bony" Tucker said he first learned about the fight when a man approached him and asked to borrow a gun. He said, "there was going to be trouble between Jim Courtwright and Luke Short." Before he could say anything else, shots rang out.

"We [Tucker and his brother] ran toward the firing, and about the time John Stewart's corner was reached, another shot was heard. Two more reports were heard in quick succession, and then a fifth and the last just as I came upon Luke Short…Fearing that he might shoot me in the excitement of the moment, I dodged around him and grabbed his pistol. It was a Colt's 45-caliber."

Jim Courtwright lay dying on the street corner, still grasping a "gun in one hand, a '45.' The chambers were full of cartridges showing that he failed to get in a shot." A later examination showed the cylinder failed to revolve.

The paper said Courtwright "was as quick, too, as lightning. It was singular then that he failed to fire his revolver at all, and it is owing beyond a doubt to the failure of his gun to operate smoothly that the tragedy was not a double one."

When questioned, Short said he was talking to Courtwright and Jake Johnson outside the White Elephant Saloon. Courtwright took offense at something he said and "immediately put his hand to his hip-pocket and pulled his [gun]. When I saw him do that, I pulled my pistol from my hip-pocket, too, and began shooting." Courtwright had three bullets in him. One through his heart, another through his shoulder, and the third broke his right thumb.

At the trial, Jake Johnson, the only witness to the shooting and a good friend to both men, testified Courtwright drew first. The shooting was ruled self-defense.

Luke Short's next gunfight occurred at the Bank Saloon in Fort Worth on December 23, 1890.

Short strode into the Bank Saloon at about 9:30. He grabbed a colored porter and forced him to walk ahead, using him as a shield while he made his way through the building. When he reached the gambling room, Short showed his revolver and commanded everyone to "skin out of here."

"Luke Short stepped out in the hall and had only proceeded a half dozen steps when the shooting took place." Witness Louie De Mouche "saw a hand extended through the door, instantly followed by the discharge of

Short's pistol." Then, a shotgun blast crashed through the window. Short took a buckshot wound in his hip; that tore through some of the outside muscles. Several of his fingers were badly injured, and his thumb was torn off at the joint.

Deputy Marshal Ben Evans arrested Charlie Wright at his saloon. Short's bullet tore through the flesh of his wrist.

When questioned, Short said, "I don't want to say much about the shooting." When asked why he fired, Short responded, "Somebody [Louis De Mouche] pulled me around just in time to see the gun go off. I do not know who held it or who did the shooting."

Charlie Wright fed authorities the same story. "I do not want to talk about the affair. I do not know who did the shooting. When asked, "How did you get your wrist hurt?" He responded, "I don't remember exactly. You see, I was a little excited."

Both men were released later that evening after posting a $1000 bond. When the affair came to trial, Wright testified, "he shot first, but that he did so because of fear from being shot by Short." Luke Short was charged with aggravated assault and fined $150.

The *Fort Worth Daily Gazette* made it seem like the public was cheated by not being presented with a dead body. The paper wrote, "Short and (Charlie) Wright are men of desperate nerve. It was expected, though, that when they did come together, there would be a case for the undertaker."

Unlike many of his contemporaries, Luke Short died in bed. He succumbed to consumption in Fort Worth, Texas, on September 20, 1893, at 39.

Bat Masterson summed up Short's life and death, saying because he was "quickest at the critical moment," he lived long enough to die in bed. "When the time came for Luke Short to pass out of this life—to render up the ghost as it were—he was able to lie down in bed in a home that was his own, surrounded by wife and friends, and peacefully await the coming end."

Gunfighter John Wesley Hardin

John Wesley Hardin was a mean, ornery, old cuss. The story is he once shot a man just for snoring.

An article published in *The Times* (Washington, DC) said Hardin was staying at a hotel in Nogales. "He was annoyed by a heavy snorer in the next room. Without making an effort to caution the sleeper, he put his ear to the thin board partition until he got the exact position of his snoring neighbor's head. Then he fired one .45 caliber bullet through the wall. The snoring stopped. The corpse was found the next morning shot through the brain."

Hardin would later say, "They tell lots of lies about me. They say I killed five or six men for snoring. Well, it ain't true! I only killed one man for snoring."

Talk about a mean son-of-a-bitch.

Hardin's autobiography, published shortly after his death, contains a laundry list of murders committed by the gunfighter. In all, Hardin took credit for killing 42 men. A more accurate number is thought to be somewhere between 20 and 25.

His first "near murder" happened at school when he was 14. Another student, Charles Sloter, accused Hardin of writing "doggerel" on the blackboard about a girl named Sal. Then he grabbed a seat next to Hardin, slugged him in the shoulder, and pulled out a knife. Sloter quickly learned he picked the wrong kid to mess with. Hardin "stabbed him twice, almost fatally in the breast." There was talk about locking him up or hanging him. Eventually, Hardin got off, but trouble seemed to follow the teen.

He killed his first man that same year. The victim, a black man named "Mage," was a former slave of his uncle, Major Holshousen. Hardin shot Mage five times and hightailed it off to his father's house to tell him what happened. His father told him to keep out of sight until things blew over. He didn't think a Southern boy could get a fair trial in post-Civil War Texas. Hardin got word three Union soldiers were hot on his trail. He could have surrendered. He could have made a run for it. Instead, he waylaid, killed the three soldiers, and buried them where no one would find them. At age fifteen, Wes Hardin had four notches in his gun.

His next kill was a gambler named Benjamin Bradley (mistakenly called Jim Bradly in his autobiography). "Bradley...tried to cut me off, getting in front of me with a pistol in one hand and a Bowie knife in the other," wrote Hardin. "He commenced to fire on me, firing once, then snapping, and then firing again. By this time, we were within five or six feet of each other, and I fired with a Remington .45 at his heart and right after that at his head."

In January of 1870, Hardin killed a circus employee at Horn Hill. Not long after that, he went to see a girl in Kosse. While he was visiting her, her sweetheart came to the door and threatened to kill him unless he gave him $100. Hardin said he lured the man to the stables with the promise of more money he had stashed in his saddlebags. The man demanded the money he had on him first. Hardin dropped some of it on the floor. When "he stooped down to pick it up, and as he was straightening up, I pulled my pistol and fired. The ball struck him between the eyes, and he fell over, a dead robber." Hardin picked up his money and hightailed it out of there.

In his autobiography, Hardin claimed he got the drop on Wild Bill Hickok when he was marshal of Abilene, but the odds are that never happened. Hardin said that when he was rolling ten pins (bowling), Wild Bill came in and asked him to take off his guns. Hardin refused. The two men walked outside to settle the matter. Bill "pulled his pistol and said: Take those pistols off. I arrest you." Hardin turned the situation around and drew down on Wild Bill.

"I told him to put his pistol up," Hardin said. Then "I cursed him for being a long-haired scoundrel that would shoot a boy with his back to him." But, instead of exchanging gunfire, they shared words. After that, they had a drink and were the best of friends.

It's all pure horse hockey and just another incidence of Hardin blowing hot air.

Hardin and his gang met up at a saloon in Comanche, Texas, on May 26, 1874, to celebrate his 21st birthday. That trip turned out to be the beginning of the end for John Wesley Hardin. Charlie Webb, a Brown County Deputy Sheriff, entered the saloon. Hardin asked if he was there to arrest him. Webb said he wasn't, so Hardin invited the deputy to have a drink. That's when all hell busted loose. Someone hollered out a warning. Hardin wheeled around just in time to see Charles Webb about to draw his pistol. "He was in the act of presenting it when I jumped to one side, drew my pistol, and fired...My aim was good, and a bullet hole in the left cheek did the work. He fell against the wall, and as he fell, he fired a second shot, which went into the air." After that, two of Hardin's friends, Jim Taylor and Bud Dixon, "pulled their pistols and fired on him [Webb] as he was falling, not knowing that I had killed him."

Now the way Hardin spun that bit of gunplay in his autobiography, Charles Webb was part of a larger plot to assassinate him. When it didn't work out the way they expected, the crowd ran outside and began to scream, "Hardin has killed Charley Webb; let us hang him."

Hardin says he immediately surrendered to Sheriff John Karnes, but when the mob went crazy, he decided to skedaddle before they stretched his neck. He bent the truth a little more, saying, "I was willing to surrender, but the sheriff said he could not protect me; the mob was too strong, and Charley Webb had been their leader. He advised me to stay around until the excitement died down and then come in and surrender."

In the days after Webb's murder, hundreds of men hit the trail to search for him. As the heat picked up, Hardin decided it was time for a fresh start. He made his way to Gainesville, Florida, and went by the name of John Swain. He moved around a lot, working as a saloonkeeper, a lumberman, and a cattleman. But, everywhere he went, trouble followed. His autobiography recounts at least eight to ten murders during this period.

The Texas Rangers captured Hardin on a Florida train on August 24, 1877. They said Hardin reached for his gun, but it got caught in his suspenders. Hardin said they took him by surprise and brutally attacked him. Whichever account is true, John Wesley Hardin wound up in prison.

After his capture, the Texas Rangers handed Hardin a pair of unloaded Colts and encouraged him to demonstrate his skills. Ranger James Gillett said Hardin manipulated the guns "with magical precision." He was a lightning-fast draw and deadly accurate. Many wild west aficionados claim Hardin was the fastest gunfighter out there, maybe even quicker than Wild Bill. But, of course, part of it could have been how he carried his guns. Hardin practiced his fast draw daily in front of a mirror and wore a special calf-skin vest with built-in holsters. That may have given him an edge. But Hardin's real secret weapon was his sleight-of-hand skills. He could manipulate a gun the way a professional gambler could handle a deck of cards.

His landlady, Mrs. Wilson, was quoted in the *El Paso Times*, published on August 23, 1895. She said Hardin was "quick as a flash; he would have a gun in each hand, clicking so fast that the clicks sounded like a rattle machine."

Hardin was sentenced to 25 years in the Huntsville Prison. While there, he studied theology and law. On February 17, 1894, he was released from prison after serving 17 years of a 25-year sentence. On July 21, Hardin passed the bar exam and was licensed to practice law in Texas.

Not long after that, he moved to El Paso and began a short reign of terror after returning to his old ways—drinking, gambling, and killing.

The lead story in the *Daily Ardmoreite* on August 20, 1895, read, "John Wesley Hardin killed Monday night at El Paso, Texas. Died with his boots on in true desperado style."

He was shot and killed at the Acme Saloon by John Selman. "At 11 o'clock tonight, Sellman stalked into the Acme with a friend, and Hardin was standing at the bar shaking dice with some friends. When he saw Sellman, he whirled around and threw his hand to his hip pocket. In an instant, Sellman's gun was out, and a ball went crashing through his brain, and while he was falling, Sellman pumped two more balls from his .44 into the man's body and then walked out and surrendered himself."

When asked why he fired as Hardin was going down, Selman said, "Good gunfighters like Wes Hardin sometimes shoot after they're hit."

John Selman deserves a separate entry in the annals of western history. He was as notorious as John Wesley Hardin. The *Austin Weekly Statesman* said Selman "did not know what fear was, and has killed not less than 20 outlaws. He was a dead shot and quick as lightning with a gun."

Surprisingly, no one bothered to mention Selman shot Hardin from behind. The bullet entered the back of his head and exited just above his right eye. Things could very well have gone the other way if Selman had met Hardin face-to-face in an old-fashioned duel.

Selman's career took him all over the board. He fought for the Confederacy during the Civil War, served as a lawman, and formed a band known as Selman's Scouts in the Lincoln County War. In late 1878, they rustled cattle and horses and murdered several innocent men. Then in 1888, he landed in El Paso, working as a professional gambler and sometimes constable. In 1894, he killed Texas Ranger Bass Outlaw after Bass killed another Texas Ranger, then turned his guns on Selman.

Ironically, Selman was shot and killed two years later in a gunfight with U. S. Deputy Marshal George Scarborough, who was killed in a gunfight not too many years later.

And, so, it goes in the west.

Doc Holliday – Frontier Gambler, Gunfighter, Sometimes Lawman

Bat Masterson spoke admiringly about most of the big-name gunfighters of the old west, but he had a particularly low opinion of Doc Holiday. "I never liked him, and few persons did," said Bat. "He had a mean disposition and differed from most of the big gunfighters in that he would seek a fight...He had few friends anywhere in the west." Virgil Earp told the *Arizona Daily Star*, "There was something peculiar about Doc...outside of us boys. I don't think he had a friend in the territory."

Although Masterson didn't come right out and call Holliday a coward, he did say, unlike Wild Bill and Wyatt Earp, who were as good with their fists as they were with their pistols, Doc Holliday was a "physical weakling." His opinion was a fifteen-year-old could make easy work of him in a "go-as-you-please fistfight." But, as soon as you put a gun in his hand, danger transformed Doc Holliday from a 98-pound weakling into a raging madman.

Like most legendary figures of the old west, much of what's been written about Doc Holliday is contradictory at best. For example, in the *Encyclopedia of Western Gunfighters* (1942), Bill O'Neal credits Doc with just two kills in a total of eight gunfights. Far from the dozens of kills and near kills most biographers attribute to him.

Doc Holliday was like a fish out of water in Dodge City and Tombstone. He was a dentist by profession but a gambler and a gunfighter by choice.

Shortly after graduating from dental school, Holliday took the equivalent of his first bullet when he learned he had contracted tuberculosis. Doctors informed him he had only a short time to live, and the best thing he could do would be to move to a drier climate. Doc took the news to heart, headed west, and set up a practice in Dallas, Texas. Not too many months after that, he gave up dentistry. Apparently, patients didn't appreciate his coughing spells. As word got around about the tubercular dentist, business dried up quicker than the weather.

It's very likely knowing that he was going to die young is what made Doc so fearless in a gunfight. Better to go out in a blaze of glory than cough your lungs out in a hospital bed. The knowledge that he would die any day probably drove Doc Holliday to the dark side—gambling, drinking, and gun fighting.

Rumor has it Doc shot up some negroes down in Georgia when he was fifteen. No one disputes there may have been some shooting, but it's unlikely anyone got themselves killed.

Doc's first known gunfight took place on January 2nd, 1875. He traded shots with a Dallas saloonkeeper named Charles Austin. No one was hurt. The *Dallas Weekly Herald* reported the two men were just blowing off steam. No actual harm was done. Both men were arrested and quickly released.

A few days later, Doc got into another scrape and killed a Dallas businessman. He hightailed it out of there one step ahead of the law and made his way to the rough-and-tumble cow town of Jacksboro, Texas.

Doc's transformation into a gunfighter took place there. He dealt poker and faro but went around armed to the hilt. He wore a gun on his hip, another in a shoulder holster, and carried a Bowie knife strapped to his leg. When he wasn't gambling or drinking, Doc practiced his draw. By all accounts, it was time well spent. Wyatt Earp told the *San Francisco Examiner* Doc was "the most skillful gambler and the nerviest, speediest, deadliest man with a six-gun I ever knew."

When Doc finally left Jacksboro, one man was dead, and several others were wounded from his three gunfights there. Keep in mind; there are no newspaper accounts or court records to back up any of these fights, just stories about Doc and his prowess with a gun.

Did those gunfights happen? Maybe. Maybe not. At this point, you may as well flip a coin. The result is likely to be just as accurate.

He moved to Denver in the winter of 1876 and tangled with a local bully named Budd Ryan. This time, the story is Ryan pulled a gun, and Doc manhandled his attacker, slashing his throat with a knife. But, again, this story is nothing more than rattlesnake snot and tumbleweed. Every account I've read says Doc couldn't have manhandled a girl scout, so the odds of him physically attacking a gun-wielding bully are beyond belief.

In July of 1877, the *Dallas Weekly Herald* reported a young man named "Doc Holliday, well known in this city, was shot and killed" by a man named Kahn. They never printed a retraction, but Doc turned up alive and breathing in Fort Griffin, Texas, several months later. The rumors of his early demise were greatly exaggerated.

Holliday first met up with Wyatt Earp in Fort Griffin, Texas, in 1877. Earp was hot on the trail of Dave Rudabaugh, and Doc tipped him off the outlaw was hiding out in Fort Davis.

Doc made his way to Dodge City in 1878 and tried his hand at dentistry, but his return to respectability was short-lived. Doc's common-law wife, Big Nose Kate, couldn't handle the quiet life and went back to whoring at a local saloon. When Doc got upset over her extracurricular activities, Big Nose Kate made herself scarce and disappeared. This time, Doc gave up dentistry for good and returned to dealing faro.

Not long after that, a group of cowboys rode into Dodge City with their guns blazing, shooting up storefronts and shop windows. After blowing off a little steam, the cowboys headed to the Long Branch Saloon, where Doc Holliday was dealing faro. The leader of the group, Ed Morrison, saw Wyatt Earp coming through the door. Morrison and the other boys drew down on him, challenging Earp to draw or die. But Doc got the drop on all of them. He ordered the cowboys to drop their guns, or they'd be wearing Morrison's brains. Doc and Wyatt quickly disarmed the cowboys and tucked them away in the Dodge City jail. It was the beginning of a beautiful friendship that would last the remainder of Doc's short life.

When things in Dodge City got a little too hot for Doc, he traveled around a bit. First, he spent some time in Leadville and Trinidad, Colorado, then Las Vegas, New Mexico Territory.

Legend has it he left a trail of dead bodies scattered along the way. While Doc was in Las Vegas, there was some talk he killed a drunk named Mike Gordon, but there is no documentation to back it up. The consensus is Gordon was drunk on his ass and started shooting up the town. Later that night, he was found all shot up and died early the next day. Because Doc was in the area, it was convenient to pin the killing on him.

Doc was involved in a string of shootings in 1879 and 1880. On March 12, 1879, he supposedly shot up Charlie White. The story is Doc ran White out of Dodge City and told him he'd kill him if he ever ran across him again. Former New Mexico Territory governor, Miguel Antonio Ontero, told reporters he saw the whole thing. Ontero said the two men faced each other down. They drew their pistols and fired, but both men missed. Scared for his life, Charlie White beat it out of town before Doc got another chance to take him down.

In October of 1880, Doc got into a disagreement with a gambler named Johnny Tyler at the Oriental Saloon. When Doc challenged him to a fight, Tyler hurried out of there. Milt Joyce, the owner of the Oriental Saloon, had Doc removed. Big mistake. Doc rushed back in a few minutes later with pistols roaring. Joyce took a bullet in the hand. William Parker, a friend of Joyce, got shot in the toe. Joyce got the last word in when he whacked Doc over the head with a pistol and knocked him out cold.

Doc appeared in court on October 12, charged with attempted murder. That should have slowed him down some, but neither Milt Joyce nor William Parker appeared as witnesses. Doc was fined twenty dollars for assault with a deadly weapon and was quickly released.

On August 13, 1881, Newman Hayes, "Old Man" Clanton, and several of his companions were shot and killed in Guadalupe Canyon while driving a herd of cattle to the Tombstone market. There's some confusion about whether Clanton was killed by a group of Mexican rustlers or a posse sent out by the Earps. Whatever happened that day, most of Tombstone blamed the killings on Doc Holliday and Warren Earp.

The situation came to a head on August 13 when Ike Clanton and Doc Holliday clashed in a drunken war of words. Doc challenged Clanton to draw, saying he was the one who drew a bead on "Old Man" Clanton. Ike Clanton was unarmed and walked away, leaving things unsettled.

The next day was a bloody mess. Three men would die in the fallout from the previous night's argument.

Ike Clanton came by Fly's boardinghouse at about 3 p.m. looking for Doc. For thirty seconds, the guns talked. Three men lay dead at the O. K. Corral when it was over. Those killed were—Billy Clanton and Frank and Tom McLaury. Ike Clanton ran away, like a scared, frightened girl, at the first sound of gunfire and lived to fight another day.

On August 19, 1884, Doc bushwhacked Billy Allen at Hyman's Saloon in Leadville, Colorado. As soon as Allen walked through the doors, Doc fired a shot that hit him in the arm. Allen fell to the floor. Doc ducked behind a cigar case and fired again, just missing Allen. The crowd quickly disarmed Doc. He was arrested, tried, and found not guilty.

Doc Holliday died in bed in Glenwood Springs, Colorado, in May of 1887. Tuberculosis had finally done what bullets couldn't.

Robert A. "Clay" Allison

Clay Allison's "trigger finger was the busiest in the early 80s," wrote the *Albuquerque Morning Journal.* "His record was twenty-one dead men, whose graves were scattered from Dodge City to Santa Fe."

The article went on to say, "Clay spent his time amusing himself shooting up small towns and dance halls and making gentlemen dance barefoot to the accompaniment of his bullets."

One of Allison's first kills was a desperado named Chunk. They met at Red River Station in New Mexico on January 7, 1874. Chunk was out to get Allison because Clay had killed his uncle.

The two men sat on opposite sides of the dinner table, each man itching for an opportunity to draw. Chunk made the first move. He dropped his knife on the floor and reached below the table to grab it. Allison didn't miss a beat—he pulled his pistol and let Chunk have it—right between the eyes. *The Evening Star* wrote, "a little red spot between Chunk's eye showed where the bullet had entered, and the man, swaying from side to side, bent gradually over and soon was perfectly still, with his face buried in the dish."

Witnesses observed Allison go on with his dinner as if nothing had happened. Then, when he finished eating, he walked out, mounted his horse, and rode away.

Marshal Sam Durnin of Pecos County, Texas, learned a lesson he'd never forget. Clay Allison was loyal to his friends—dead or alive.

Durnin killed one of Allison's friends in a "honakatonk" melee. When Clay learned about it, he vowed to show the marshal a thing or two. Two months later, things came to a head in Curt Munson's saloon. Durnin wasn't taking any chances. He hid in a back room of the saloon for a full half-hour, keeping Allison covered with his Winchester. Finally, Durnin walked up to Allison and pointed a .45 at his heart when he couldn't take the suspense any longer.

"Like the dab of a cat's paw, Allison reached out and caught the wrist of Durnin's hand that held the gun. A man of bull's strength, he leaped over the table and twisted that wrist of Durnin's until the marshal had to drop the gun to the floor and gasp with pain."

Allison kicked the gun out of the marshal's reach as he snatched his other gun out of its holster. "Then Allison put his knee in the small of the helpless marshal's back, grabbed him from behind by both ears, kneed him forward and out of the saloon, and in that way, he prodded Marshal Sam Durnin, a bad man himself, all over the streets of Durango."

The *Washington Evening Star* wrote Durnin survived the night, but the humiliation he suffered that day dogged him for the remainder of his life.

Another time in Las Animas, Allison was drunk and whirling his revolver around his finger at a dancehall. For one reason or another, he got a bug up his butt and screamed for everyone to take their hats off. Most men complied, knowing Allison's reputation for being a homicidal maniac when drinking.

Deputy Marshal Mace Bowman wasn't ready to give in so easily. He told Clay, "all the Allison's in Tennessee couldn't make him take his hat off."

Things got so quiet after that; you could've heard a mouse fart. Allison sipped on his whisky as the crowd began to edge away.

"Let's lay our guns on the bar and take our places across the room," Allison challenged Mace. "At the word, each man goes for his gun. The one that doesn't get there first is out of luck."

They laid their revolvers on the bar with muzzles crossed.

At the word, "Bowman sprang across the room like a panther," said the report in the *Yorkville Enquirer*. Allison found the muzzles of both revolvers in his face.

"How do you like the color of it?" asked Bowman.

"It's all right, Mace," said Allison, throwing up his hands. "You're the best man."

That was the end of it. Both men had another drink and walked away.

Like most western bad men, many good and bad things were said about Clay Allison—most of them published after his death, so he had no say in setting the record straight.

New Mexico cattleman Frank Councelle said Clay Allison was "one of the worst men that ever saddled a cayuse in the Pecos country of Texas." However, the *Yorkville Enquirer* took Allison's side, writing, "There was a long list of casualties to Clay Allison's pistol, but they all occurred in face-to-face encounters, with no working up of the drop or any unfair advantage on his part."

By all accounts, Allison was a good-hearted man, a steady friend, and a homicidal drunk. Smart men—who wanted to live would steer clear of Allison when he was on a bender.

On election day in Cimarron, Allison hung around the polls all day. When the polls closed, he began drinking with a group of fellows at Lambert's barroom. Allison pulled his revolver and bashed a man named Caton over the head. "No explanations were asked or offered." The man carried out was a bloody mess.

In 1878, Allison took down a Mexican named Pancho in the same bar. The two men stood in a corner. Pancho held his sombrero in his hand in front of him while he talked to Allison. While he talked, Pancho was inching his hand down towards his pistol. Allison played the Mexican, giving Pancho plenty of time to think he would be able to make his move. Seconds later, Allison reached for his guns. Two shots rang out. The lights in the barroom went dark during the fight and were never relit. Allison was seen to get on his horse and ride away. Everyone else headed home.

When Lambert arrived at the bar the following day, he noticed Pancho asleep in a chair. Or, at least, he thought he was sleeping. But, when he tried to wake him, Lambert discovered the Mexican was dead—with one bullet in his head and another in his heart.

Another man said to have met his maker at the muzzle of Clay Allison's revolver was Charles Faber, a city marshal of Las Animas. The marshal dropped Allison's brother with a shotgun, and before he could make his getaway, Clay let him have it. And, as if he hadn't made his point by killing the man, he dragged the dead body over to where his brother lay bleeding and told him, "Here's the fellow that shot you."

As he aged, Allison became more philosophical. The *Anaconda Standard* reported he met an old enemy in town, and rather than take off shooting, they drank and talked about politics and cattle as they toasted each other. Then, finally, the conversation turned to baptism. Although Allison said he favored sprinkling, the other man insisted immersion was the best method to be saved. Then he called Allison some names and reached for his pistol.

"Perhaps Allison was not posted on theological questions," said the reporter, but he "was adept with a .45, and he killed his antagonist before he had his gun in a position to shoot."

Not long after that incident, Allison found religion of a sort.

He married the widow McSwayne, who had a large spread about twenty miles outside Cimarron. He gave up drink and gunplay and became a respectable cattleman from then on. Newspaper accounts after that talk about his business acumen and how he held out for this or that price. He soon had a herd of over ten thousand cattle, making him one of the wealthiest ranchers.

Clay Allison died four or five years later after falling from a freighter's six-mule wagon. The wheels passed over his head and crushed the life out of him.

For most of his life, he lived by the gun, driven by liquor to gunplay, misdeeds, and murder. When he was free of the drink, he was the good-humored friend everyone wanted to be around. But, after he had a few drinks, Allison transformed into a demon—sometimes playful, more often deadly.

The St. John's Herald pegged Allison best when they quipped, "Clay was a good friend and a bad enemy."

Western Lawmen

Lawmen often straddled the line between good and evil in the wild west. In many situations, it was impossible to distinguish the good guy from the bad guy. *The Opelousas Courier* said, "it was a common custom in the west to select a sheriff who made a record as a killer."

Doc Holliday was a notorious gambler but quick to join a posse when the call went out.

Wild Bill served as a city marshal of Hays City, Kansas, and later as a marshal of Abilene, Kansas. But in real life, Wild Bill was a badass gambler and gunman, rumored to have started over 100 men on their journey to perdition.

Wild Bill "was the quickest, surest shot ever in the West," wrote the *Saint Paul Daily Globe*. "He had killed nearly forty men in his time, 'not including Indians and greasers,' as the bad men used pleasantly to say. It was the rarest thing that he shot his victim more than once. His favorite spot in which to plant his deadly bullet was between the eyes." At one time, he was an excellent lawman. But "woman, whisky, and faro proved the ruin of Wild Bill."

Wyatt Earp, and his brothers, Virgil, Morgan, and James, are best remembered as lawmen, but they were anything but angels during their lifetime. During the O. K. Corral gunfight, the Earps and Doc Holliday brutally shot down James Clanton and Frank, and Tom McLaury. After Morgan's death, the Earps rode out dead set upon vengeance and killed Frank Stillwell, Florentino Cruz, and three other men they suspected were involved in his murder.

The Dalton brothers began their careers as lawmen but soon turned into outlaws.

Tom Horn may have been a cattle detective, but his idea of bringing his man to justice didn't have anything to do with courts or justice. He had a more permanent solution in mind. Criminals who faced him ended up planted six feet underground.

There was something about the west that messed with a man's mind. So many times, there was no right or wrong. Justice came down to which side of the tracks you found yourself on at a particular moment.

Another truth, reported in *The Opelousas Courier*, was, "when a man accepted the marshal's star or service badge, he knew pretty well that he was taking long chances in a game with death." A silver star glowed like a target over the marshal's heart.

It was an invitation to drunken fools, gunfighter wannabes, and men seeking a reputation. By killing the marshal or sheriff, many felt they'd share his power. It was like the ancient Indian civilizations where warriors ate the hearts of their dead enemies—it transferred their strength, power, and cunning to them.

Wild Bill – James Butler Hickok

Henry M. Stanley interviewed Wild Bill for a series of articles published in the *St. Louis Democrat* in April 1867. He wrote Wild Bill "stands six foot one inch in his moccasins and is as handsome a specimen of man as could be found." He "held himself straight, and had broad compact, shoulders, was large chested, with small waist, and well-formed muscular limbs."

Stanley asked, "I say, Mr. Hickok, how many men have you killed to your certain knowledge?"

"After a little deliberation, he replied, 'I suppose I have killed considerable over a hundred.'"

"What made you kill all those men? Did you kill them without cause or provocation?"

"No, by heaven, I have never killed one man without good cause."

Later in the interview, Wild Bill described his first kill to Stanley.

He was lying in bed in a hotel room in Leavenworth, Kansas, when he heard a commotion outside his door. Bill grabbed his six-shooter and a Bowie knife and remained under his covers. "The door was opened, and five men entered the room. I kept perfectly still until just as the knife touched my breast, I sprang aside and buried mine in his heart and used my revolver on the others right and left." As soon as the shooting stopped, Bill ran out of the room and didn't stop until he reached Fort Leavenworth.

James Butler Hickok earned the moniker "Wild Bill" in an 1862 showdown with Davis McCandles, his brother William, and several of their hired hands. The boys caught up with Wild Bill at the stage station and demanded he pay up on a debt he owed them. Unfortunately, the talk soon turned to gunplay, and when it was over, the two McCandles brothers, and one of their accomplices, lay dead in the street.

The *Atchison Daily Champion* reported, "Wild Bill...shot McKandles through the heart with a rifle, and then stepping out of doors, revolver in hand, shot another one of the gang dead; severely wounded a third...and slightly wounded the fourth."

When the fighting was over, and Bill had finished nursing his wounds, he told friends, "I just got wild and slashed about like a bear with a death wound." The next thing you know, James Butler Hickok became known everywhere as Wild Bill.

After the McCandles fight, Bill made his way to Leavenworth, Kansas, where he became a Brigade Wagon Master for General John Charles Fremont, trucking supplies out of Fort Leavenworth. In 1863, he worked as a Union spy, gathering information behind the Confederate lines.

At the end of the Civil War, Wild Bill drifted into Missouri and faced down Davis Tutt in the Town Square of Springfield, Missouri, on July 21, 1865. It was one of the classic gunfights pictured in every western film since the beginning of time. The two men stood fifteen paces apart, staring each other down in the hot sun. Finally, they reached for their guns. One man fell dead in the street. The other walked away.

Here's how it started.

Wild Bill and Tutt sat across from each other, engaged in a high-stakes card game. Bill won a big hand, and Tutt reminded him he owed him some money. Bill paid up. A few moments later, Tutt brought up another debt Hickok owed him. After a quarrel over the amount owed, Tutt grabbed Wild Bill's gold pocket watch and said he'd hang on to it until Bill settled the debt.

Wild Bill challenged Tutt to a duel in the town square. According to an account published in the February 1867 issue of *Harper's New Monthly Magazine*, "Tutt then showed his pistol. Bill kept a sharp eye on him, and before Tutt could Pint it, Bill had his'n out.

"At that moment, you could have heard a pin drop in that squar. Both Tutt and Bill fired, but one discharge followed the other so quick that it's hard to say which went off first. Tutt was a famous shot, but he missed this time; the ball from the pistol went over Bill's head. The instant Bill fired, without waiting ter see of he had hit Tutt, he wheeled on his heels and pointed his pistol at Tutt's friends, who had already drawn their weapons."

Wild Bill earned his reputation as a fast-gun that day.

Bill entered a country saloon in Jefferson County, Missouri, in 1867. Five cowboys picked a fight with him. One of the boys snuck up behind Bill, gave him a shove that made him spill his beer, and almost sent him tumbling to the ground. Bill wheeled around, bloodied the cowboy's nose, and sent him crashing to the floor.

Then he challenged four of them to a duel outside. Bill shot one of them right off but took a ball in his arm. Then, in an instant, he shifted his gun to the other hand and dropped the other three. Four men lay dead in the street, another severely wounded.

On September 8, 1869, Bill was elected city marshal of Hays City, Kansas, one of the toughest towns on the frontier. Shortly after, Sam Strangham approached Wild Bill at a local saloon and pulled his Navy Colt. Bill got off the first shot and fired his derringer into Strangham's left eye. "The man was stone dead on his feet, falling forward onto his face without even a twitch of the muscles."

Later, in December 1869, a bully named Bill Mulvey went on a wild, drunken bender, terrorizing the town—breaking windows with a club, threatening the townspeople, and reportedly chasing two constables to the city limits. After that, Mulvey got the drop on Wild Bill, holding two pistols to his head. Bill faked him out by telling an imaginary constable behind him not to kill him. Mulvey turned to look, and Wild Bill blew his brains out.

On February 12, 1870, Wild Bill had a tussle with some soldiers from the Seventh Cavalry at Paddy Welch's Saloon. He killed several of the soldiers and wounded a few more. During the fight, Bill took seven balls in his arms and legs before he could hightail it out of town. After his recovery, Wild Bill was forced to lay low because General Sheridan had put out an order to bring him in "dead or alive." Several months later, after the Seventh Cavalry pulled out of Fort Hays, Bill returned to Kansas and was appointed marshal of Abilene.

On October 7, 1871, the *Junction City Union* reported a gunfight in the Alamo, "a gambling hell." City Marshal Wild Bill "fired with marvelous rapidity and characteristic accuracy." Several men, including Phil Cole and Jack Harvey, were shot and killed. A policeman, Jim McWilliams, rushed in to help, and Bill accidentally shot and killed him.

After the accidental killing of McWilliams, Bill hung up his guns and turned to acting. In the fall of 1872, he joined Buffalo Bill, and Texas Jack in a series of western reenactments staged by dime-novelist Ned Buntline. Then, in 1873 – 1874 he joined Buffalo Bill to perform in his "Scouts of the Plains." But, Buffalo Bill said, Wild Bill wasn't much of an actor, either. Every time he "went up on the stage before an audience, it was almost impossible for him to utter a word."

In 1876, Bill tried his luck at mining in the Black Hills. Eventually, he wound up in Deadwood, Dakota Territory, where he spent much of his time gambling in Nuttal & Mann's Saloon. Around 3:00 p.m. on August 2, 1876, Bill played poker with his back to the door, something he rarely did. Jack McCall sidled up behind Wild Bill, and before anyone could see what he was doing, McCall pulled out a large pistol. "The ball went crashing through the back of Bill's head and came out at the center of his right cheek…Wild Bill dropped his head forward; the cards fell from his relaxing grip, and, in a succession of slow movements, he slipped out of the chair and fell prone upon the floor."

The man who claimed to have killed over one hundred men lay dead on the floor. His final hand, a pair of aces and eights, became known as the "dead man's hand."

Wyatt Earp – Frontier Lawman

Bat Masterson said Wyatt Earp "more than any man I have ever known was devoid of physical fear." He said Earp was a "terror in action, either with his fists or a gun."

In 1877, the *Dodge City Times* wrote Wyatt Earp "had a quiet way of taking the most desperate characters into custody which invariably gave one the impression that the city was able to enforce her mandates and preserve her dignity." The paper said, "It wasn't considered policy to draw a gun on Wyatt unless you got the drop and meant to burn powder without any preliminary talk."

The meaning was clear. If you were on the business end of a 45, dealing with Wyatt Earp, you'd soon need a reservation at Boot Hill.

In October 1878, Wyatt assisted in the arrest of James Kennedy for the murder of Dora Hand, alias Fannie Keenan.

Four pistol shots rang out in a Dodge City saloon shortly after 4 a.m. James Kennedy ran out of the saloon, jumped on his horse, and galloped down the road, heading towards the fort.

The next afternoon, Wyatt Earp, Jim Masterson, Marshal Basset, and William Tilghman rode off in pursuit. They started down the river road and halted at a ranch below the fort.

The next day they were slowed down by a colossal storm, during which it rained and hailed all day. They took up the trail again the next day and waited at a ranch near Meade City. Marshal Basset was sure they were ahead of their man, so the posse milled about, trying to look inconspicuous.

At about 4 p.m., a solitary rider appeared on the distant plain. "The cautious manner in which he approached the camp led the officers to believe that he snuffled [sniffed out] the danger from every movement forward." The rider halted a few hundred yards from the camp. It appeared to the posse as if he dreaded coming any closer.

Sensing that he wouldn't ride any closer, the posse hollered for him to "Throw his hands up!" For a moment, it looked as if he was going to turn and run. The posse fired several shots in quick succession, instantly killing the man's horse.

When the posse captured Kennedy, they discovered a carbine, two pistols, and a knife.

By the end of 1879, Wyatt Earp, his brothers Morgan and Virgil, and Doc Holliday made their way to Tombstone,

Arizona. Unfortunately, since their arrival in Tombstone, the Earps had nursed a feud with the Clantons.

It came to a head in late August 1881.

"Tuesday night Ike Clanton and Doc Holliday had some difficulty in the Alhambra saloon," wrote the *Arizona Weekly Citizen*. "Hard words passed between them, and it was assumed next time they met, there would be trouble."

That was an understatement.

The next day, Ike Clanton strode down the street armed with a revolver and a rifle. Wyatt Earp disarmed him. In court later that morning, Earp challenged Clanton to "get his crowd" and get ready for a fight.

At about 2 p.m., crowds gathered on the corners of Allen and Fourth Streets, waiting for the expected fight to break out.

Sheriff Behan ordered Wyatt Earp to disarm his posse.

The Earps continued to walk down Fremont Street. Behan shouted at Earp, warning him not to go. He had disarmed the men waiting at the corral.

Earp kept walking.

He yelled out to the men in the O. K. Corral. "Throw up your hands, boys; I intend to disarm you."

Frank McLaury made a move to draw his revolver. Wyatt drew first and let him have it in the belly. Doc Holliday blasted Tom McLaury in the side at that same moment, using a short Wells Fargo-style shotgun he had concealed under his coat.

Billy Clanton got off a shot that tore into Morgan Earp's shoulder. Morgan fell to the ground, rose, and got several shots fired off after Frank McLaury, as he attempted to escape up Fremont Street.

Doc fired two more balls after Frank McLaury. His shots were deadly, as always. One hit McLaury in the temple, the other in the chest.

Billy Clanton shot Virgil Earp in the right leg.

Ike Clanton ran like his ass was catching on fire. The *Arizona Weekly Citizen* said, "he ran through the O. K. Corral, across Allen Street into Kellogg's saloon, and thence into Toughnut Street, where he was arrested and taken to the county jail."

Thirty shots were fired off in less than 25 seconds. Three men lay dead on the streets near the O.K. Corral.

More than any other, it was a day that would define the violence that besieged the old west.

An uneasy peace followed the shootout.

Ike Clanton took his case to court and filed murder charges against the Earps and Doc Holliday. After two months of heated testimony, Judge Spicer determined there wasn't enough evidence to charge the Earps.

Virgil Earp got ambushed walking down Allen Street in Tombstone in late December. Several months later, Morgan Earp got killed shooting billiards at Campbell and Hatch's Saloon. He leaned over to take a shot when two pistol shots rang out.

That was on March 17, 1882.

Three days later, Frank Stillwell, one of the men responsible for Morgan's death, lay dead outside the train depot in Tucson, Arizona.

Allen Hinckley was standing near the depot around 7:15 p.m. He remembered seeing six quick flashes and a crowd of six to ten men standing near the body. J. W. Evans watched Doc Holliday get off the cars. He had a shotgun in each hand and walked towards the railroad office. Not long after that, he watched him return without any weapons.

Several minutes later, Doc hooked up with Wyatt at Porter's Hotel. When Virgil Earp joined them, they started walking towards the depot. Doc had an "Ulster over his shoulder and a shotgun concealed under it. The Earps had short Wells Fargo shotguns."

They boarded the train and walked towards the rear of the sleeper. Two shots were fired in the head of the train, followed by five more in quick succession.

The grand jury ruled that Frank Stillwell died from "gunshot wounds inflicted by Wyatt Earp, Warren Earp,

Sherman McMasters, J. H. Holliday, and Johnson, whose first name is unknown."

The *Seattle Post Intelligencer* wrote, "When Stillwell's body was found, it was so riddled with bullets that it would have made a very good sieve."

After killing Stillwell, the Earp posse made a brief stop back in Tombstone, most likely searching for Pete Spence, another of the men indicted for killing Morgan Earp. Sheriff Behan attempted to disband the Earp party, but the heavily armed posse pushed past him. Behan shrugged his shoulders and let them ride out. Unfortunately, there wasn't much he could do. He didn't have the firepower to stop them.

The Earp party rode towards Pete Spence's ranch in the south pass of the Dragoons. Theodore Judah testified he was ranching in the Dragoons when the Earp party stopped him. They questioned him concerning the whereabouts of Pete Spence and Florentino Cruz, then rode off. Not much later, shots rang out over the hill in the direction the posse headed.

Judah said the "shooting did not last over twenty seconds." The shots rang out, "one after another in quick succession." He thought he heard ten or twelve shots altogether.

The next day, Judah discovered Florentino Cruz dead near Pete Spence's ranch in the south pass of the

Dragoons. Dr. G. E. Goodfellow testified he found four bullets in the body. One in the right temple (that penetrated the brain), one in the right shoulder, one on the right side of the body near the liver, and another in the left thigh. So he was confident the wound in the thigh was inflicted after Cruz died.

On March 24, 1882, the Earp party engaged in what would later be called the Battle of Burleigh Springs. Wyatt Earp, Warren Earp, Sherman McMasters, Doc Holliday, and Texas Jack faced a dangerous group of "cowboys" led by "Curly Bill" Brocius.

Burleigh Springs rests about eight miles outside of Tombstone. The Earps rode towards the spring from the east and dismounted.

They said nine men rode in from nowhere and began shooting at them. The Earps ducked for cover, regrouped, and charged their attackers—throwing up a murderous fire. One of the cowboys went down.

The "cowboys" ran toward the brush, jumped on their horses, and sped off toward Charleston. The man killed by the Earp party was Curly Bill Brocius, who had killed Marshal White of Tombstone the previous September.

Legend has it Wyatt Earp took seven bullets through his clothes that day but didn't receive a single scratch. Sherman McMasters took one shot through his clothes, and Texas Jack's horse was shot dead under him.

Altogether, the Earp party killed four men in their desperate search for the murderers of Morgan Earp. Pete Spence escaped their grasp by turning himself into Sheriff Behan. A year later, he was imprisoned for pistol-whipping a suspect while he was a deputy sheriff in Georgetown, New Mexico. He received a five-year sentence in the Tombstone Arizona Territorial Penitentiary for that killing.

The *San Francisco Daily Record Union* said the Earp party was "composed of desperate men, who will fight to the death, and it is stated they have all been sworn in as Deputy United States Marshals, in which case they will have the color of law under which to act."

Like Bat Masterson, Wyatt Earp became involved in sporting events and boxing matches in the 1890s.

In 1896, he refereed the Sharkey- Fitzimmons fight. Manager Gibbs of the National Club said Earp was selected because Sharkey and Fitzimmons could not agree on a choice. Because they couldn't decide, it fell to the club to choose a referee. Gibbs told the press, "I knew Wyatt Earp was a cool, clear-headed person of unimpeachable reputation and one who would be perfectly fair to both fighters." Besides, he reasoned, Earp had refereed thirty previous bouts. What was one more?

As soon as Earp was chosen to referee the bout, rumors circulated that the contest was fixed. Wyatt Earp awarded the $10,000 purse to Thomas Sharkey because of a foul by Robert Fitzimmons. When doctors examined Sharkey after the bout, they said his injuries did not incapacitate him—therefore, a foul was not warranted. Fitzimmons filed suit against Wyatt Earp, Thomas Sharkey, and the National Athletic Club for corruption, collusion, and fraud.

The day after the fight, officials arrested Earp for carrying a concealed weapon without a permit. He got off on that one, but they discovered a connection between him and one of Sharkey's backers—a horserace promoter named Dan Lynch.

In August 1897, Wyatt Earp followed the flood of gold seekers into Alaska. He built the Dexter Saloon in Nome, Alaska, with Charlie Hoxie. It was a lavish spot, the fanciest and most luxurious in the city at the time. Downstairs, men could grab a drink and roll their money on dice and card games. There were twelve rooms upstairs for those seeking more intimate pleasures.

In 1899, Wyatt Earp left Alaska, headed towards Seattle, then Tonopah, Nevada, where he worked as a saloonkeeper and hotel owner. In 1910, he became a part-time police officer in Los Angeles. The following year, the tables were turned on him, and the Los Angeles Police Department arrested Earp for running a crooked faro game.

Wyatt Earp died on January 13, 1929. He was eighty years old and desperate to get his story told the way he wanted. Finally, in 1931, Stuart Lake wrote the first full-scale biography of Wyatt Earp, titled *Wyatt Earp: Frontier Marshal*. More than anything else, that book transformed Earp into the legendary lawman we know him as today.

If not for it, this 1882 quote from the *Tombstone Epitaph* more likely would have best characterized Wyatt Earp. "In their dealings with the so-called cowboys, they [the Earps] have forgotten that they were peace officers and constituted themselves as executioners...In our opinion...were all official authority taken from the hands of the Earp brothers, there would be comparative peace in Tombstone unless they became mere desperadoes, as is possible."

The truth is Wyatt Earp was nothing but a two-bit conman, elevated into national folklore shortly after his death. He was brave. He possessed plenty of nerve but played fast and loose with the law—twisting it to fit his ever-changing circumstances.

"Bat" Masterson – This Western Lawman Outlived Them All

Today, we think of Bat Masterson as a frontier good guy, but in his day, the press wasn't sure which side of the law Bat was on. The *Globe Republican* (Dodge City) wrote, "Bat is one of the best-known sports in the West and has had a checkered career ever since he came into prominence as a city marshal of Dodge City when it was a cowboy town."

Years later, in 1905, when Masterson became a deputy marshal in New York on the recommendation of Teddy Roosevelt, the *Washington Times* suggested his selection was a bit of absurd overkill. They said, "The action is somewhat similar to that of Congress when it passed a $50,000,0000 appropriation bill for national defenses and called it a 'peace measure,' shortly after the blowing up of the Battleship Maine."

Or, maybe it was an extension of Theodore Roosevelt's trademark phrase, "speak softly, and carry a big stick." Only the *Times* understood you couldn't fight criminals by inviting a killer to the party. So appointing Bat Masterson as a deputy marshal was like throwing down a challenge to the criminal class, especially if you factored in Bat's troubled past.

William Barclay Masterson made his way to the Kansas Frontier in 1871 at the tender young age of eighteen. He worked as a buffalo hunter, a civilian scout for General Nelson A. Miles in his Indian campaigns, and not too many years later as a frontier lawman.

In 1874, Bat took part in the Second Battle of Adobe Walls—an epic standoff between 27 buffalo hunters and 700 Comanche, Cheyenne, Kiowa, and Arapaho warriors.

Adobe Walls was an obscure trading post in the middle of the Texas Panhandle. At the time of the fight, it consisted of three haphazard buildings—Frederick Leonard's store, James Hanrahan's saloon, and Tom O'Keefe's blacksmith shop.

In the late spring of 1874, buffalo hunters invaded the Llano Estacado and killed over 100,000 buffalo in a short period. The Indians, led by Quanah Parker, pushed back over the loss of their food supply. They first attacked a small hunter's camp, then moved on to Adobe Walls.

The warriors split off into four separate bands. One group struck O'Keefe's blacksmith shop, which had four men, and a woman hidden inside.

Ten men barricaded themselves inside Hanrahan's building, seven armed with Buffalo fifty caliber guns. James Hanrahan passed the order not to fire until the Indians came within 30 yards.

Another band rushed Frederick Leonard's building, where the door stood wide open when the attack started. At the first shot, Leonard ran into his store. Sam Smith made it inside just as the doors were slammed shut. Close behind him were Quanah Parker and 25 warriors who slammed their bodies against the door but couldn't break it down.

Ike and Shorty Shadler slept in their wagon north of the stockade, unaware the Indians had laid siege to Adobe Walls. The Indians snuck up on the two men, killed and scalped them as they slept, then scalped the brother's dog for good measure.

At Adobe Walls, 25 warriors rode up to O'Keefe's, dismounted, and rushed the building. The men inside opened fire. Across the way, Billy Dixon and Bat Masterson poured a deadly fire into the attackers from their position at Hanrahan's store.

Despite their mounting losses, the Indians continued to charge the building in small groups of two to five for most of the day.

On day two of the siege, the defenders abandoned Hanrahan's place and split up among the other buildings.

Later that night, a hunter named Reed volunteered for a suicide mission. After dark, he raced out of the building and made a mad dash toward Dodge City to summon help.

Beginning at sunrise on the third day, the Indians launched a series of small attacks. William Olds was killed by one of his guns during one of the charges. He fell through a trap door on the roof and landed dead at his wife's feet.

By 5 a.m. on the fourth day of the siege, 100 buffalo hunters arrived to reinforce Adobe Walls.

On July 14, the Indian warriors lifted the siege and rode away. The hunters didn't waste any time getting out of there. They set out on foot for Dodge City. Eighty Indians, four white men, and 200 Indian ponies lay dead on the battlefield.

Years later, the *Salt Lake Herald* shared this story about Bat Masterson at Adobe Walls. A man named Shepherd tried to shoot an Indian "six times and missed him every time." Having no success, he asked Bat to give it a whirl.

"I saw Mr. Indian breaking my way," said Bat, "getting out of range of fire from Bob Wright's store. I commenced getting a bead on him. As he backed an inch or two more, I let fly, and Mr. Indian bounded in the air about 3 feet, dropped his rifle, and fell dead."

And, with that shot, Bat Masterson stepped on the stage into frontier history.

Masterson's first recorded kill occurred at the Lady Gay saloon in Sweetwater, Texas, on the evening of January 24, 1876. He played poker with Harry Fleming, Jim Duffy, and Corporal Melvin King. King soon left, apparently frustrated, because he was losing.

Bat, Charlie Norton, and a working girl named Mollie Brennan walked across the street to Charlie Norton's dance hall. Someone pounded on the door. Bat went to answer it. Melvin King pushed his way in—revolver in hand, cursing at Bat. Mollie quickly jumped between the two men just as King pulled the trigger. His first bullet missed Mollie and hit Masterson smack dab in the belly. King's second shot sent Mollie tumbling to the floor—dead. That bought Bat the time he needed to pull his pistol. Melvin King hit the floor—fatally wounded.

The shooting was quickly ruled self-defense. Bat never had much to say about it. In 1881, he told the *Kansas City Journal*, "I had a little difficulty with some soldiers down there, but never mind; I dislike to talk about it."

By early June 1877, Bat found himself in another scrape in Dodge City. "Robert Gilmore was making a talk for himself in a rather emphatic manner, to which Marshal Deger took exceptions and started for the dog house [jail] with him. Bobby walked very leisurely—so much so that Larry felt it necessary to administer a few personal kicks. This was soon interrupted by Bat Masterson, who wound his arm affectionately around the marshal's neck and let the prisoner escape." Deger then got in a row with Bat.

Joe Mason grabbed Bat's gun. Bat did his damnedest to get another one from the crowd. Finally, seeing that the marshal was in trouble, several cowboys came to his aid and held Bat down. That "gave him [marshal Deger] a chance to draw his gun and beat bat over the head until blood flew" all over.

The *Dodge City Times* reported, "Bat Masterson seemed possessed of extraordinary strength, every inch of the way was closely contested, but the city dungeon was reached at last, and in he went. If he had got hold of his gun before going in, there would have been a general killing."

Ironically, the same issue of the *Dodge City Times* that featured Bat's arrest announced his brother Ed's appointment as assistant marshal of Dodge City. The paper said, "He is not very large, but there are not many men who would be anxious to tackle him a second time. He makes a good officer."

In early November 1877, Bob Shaw got it into his head to take Texas Dick down a few bars at the Lone Star Saloon. When Ed Masterson entered the saloon, he discovered Bob Shaw with "a huge pistol in one hand and a hogshead of blood in his right eye, ready to relieve Texas Dick of his existence in this world."

Ed tried to find a peaceful solution. "Officer Masterson then gently tapped the belligerent Shaw upon the back of the head with the butt of his shooting iron, merely to convince him of the vanities of this frail world and to teach him that all isn't lovely." The smack on the head "didn't have the desired effect, and instead of dropping, as any man of fine sensibilities would have done, Shaw turned his battery [gun] upon the officer and let him have it in the right breast." The shot knocked Ed's right arm out of commission, but as he fell, he got off a few well place shots with his left hand, hitting Shaw in the "left hand and left leg."

Texas Dick took a bullet to the groin, "making a painful and dangerous, though not necessarily a fatal wound." Frank Buskirk got too close to the action and took a bullet to his left arm.

In the end, the *Dodge City Times* reported, "Nobody was killed, but for a time, it looked as though the undertaker and the coroner would have something to do." The paper commended Deputy Marshal Masterson for his bravery.

Later that same month, on November 24, 1877, Bat Masterson was elected sheriff of Ford County, Kansas. The *Dodge City Times* described the new sheriff as "cool, decisive, and a bad man with a pistol."

The *New York Times* later commented, "It took a man with a reputation to be sheriff of Ford County." If that was the case, Bat Masterson was a perfect choice.

Dodge City was still a rough-and-tumble cattle town in those days. Cowboys ruled Dodge City from July to November when they drove the big herds into town fresh off the Chisolm Trail. When they arrived in Dodge City, the cowboys needed to blow off some steam. Many rode into the city—firing six-shooters and rifles into the air. After they disposed of their horses, most of the cowboys walked off searching for drinks, smokes, and some close companionship from a dancehall girl.

Shortly after 10 p.m. on April 9, 1878, shots rang out from the south side of the tracks. Deputy Marshal Ed Masterson and policeman Haywood rushed to the scene and found six cowboys newly arrived in town. Masterson discovered that one of the cowboys, Jack Wagner, was carrying a six-shooter contrary to city ordinance. He disarmed the man and turned the weapon over to the cattle boss, A. M. Walker.

Later that same evening, Masterson met Wagner outside a dance hall and noticed he was again carrying a pistol. He attempted to take it from him. Policeman Haywood rushed forward to assist, but as he did, several cowboys shoved a gun in his face and held him back.

Someone fired a shot into his face, but luckily for officer Haywood, it misfired.

Seconds later, Wagner fired a round into Ed Masterson's abdomen. Five shots followed in quick succession.

Jack Wagner staggered into Peacock's saloon—gut shot. He would soon die from the wound. A. W. Walker, Wagner's trail boss, took a bullet in his left lung and several more in his right arm. He escaped into Peacock's saloon and was left for dead.

Ed Masterson went across the street to Hoover's saloon, staggered up to George Hinkle, and told him, "George, I'm shot!" The *Leavenworth Weekly Times* reported, "His clothes were still on fire from the discharge of the pistol, which had been placed against the right side of his abdomen and 'turned loose,' making a hole large enough for the introduction of the whole pistol. The ball passed completely through him, leaving him no possible chance for life."

The big question is: Who shot Jack Wagner and A. M. Walker? Legend tells us it was Bat Masterson. *Years later, the Arizona Republican* wrote, Bat killed the seven men responsible for his brother's death in as many minutes. The murderers locked the doors to the saloon when they saw him coming. "Masterson jumped square against the door with both feet bursting it open at the first attempt. Then sprang inside, firing immediately right and left. Four dropped dead in a shorter time than it requires to tell it." The other three outlaws ran for their horses, trying desperately to escape. "Before they reached the outskirts of the town, all three had bitten the dust."

It's a great story!

But guess what? It never happened. I read every newspaper account published in 1878 that mentioned the Mastersons, and Bat's name didn't come up one time as having avenged Ed. Not once!

Instead, most of the published newspaper accounts left things rather vague. All three participants stagger away into nearby saloons to take their final curtain call. But all we know for sure is that six gunshots rang out quickly. Jack Wagner nailed Ed Masterson. But who shot Wagner and Walker remains a mystery. All the stories implied that Ed Masterson took down his killers before he died. But that's as far as it goes. The real story is anyone's guess.

In mid-April of 1881, Bat got in a tangle with A. J. Peacock and Al Updegraff on the main streets in Dodge City. The *Las Vegas Morning Gazette* said, "the cause was a private quarrel." Bat's brother Jim was a partner in the Lady Gay Dance Hall and Saloon with A. J. Peacock. Peacock hired his brother-in-law, Al Updegraff, as a bartender, against the wishes of Jim Masterson. In no time, the matter escalated, and Bat found himself rushing back to Dodge City to protect his brother Jim.

The way it all played out, Bat arrived in town by train on April 16, 1881. Suspecting there might be foul play, he slipped out of the train just before it pulled into the depot. As he rounded the corner by the depot, Bat encountered Updegraff and Peacock. Gunfire soon broke out, and for several minutes downtown, Dodge City sounded like a war zone.

Mayor Webster and Marshal Singer eventually arrested Bat. He was fined $8.00 and another $2.00 for court costs and allowed to leave town, along with his brother Jim.

When he left, it was evident Bat had worn out his welcome. The *Dodge City Times* made it clear Bat Masterson was persona non-grata. "The firing on the street by Bat Masterson, and jeopardizing the lives of citizens, is severely condemned by our people, and the good opinion many citizens had of Bat has been changed to one of contempt."

In 1883, New York Police Superintendent Thomas Byrnes summoned Bat. One of the city's prominent millionaires, George Gould, was being shadowed by a suspicious character, and the city's detectives weren't having any luck catching him. Superintendent Byrnes said he chose Bat because he "would not be afraid to shoot a man on a crowded Broadway and who would be certain to hit the right man."

Bat pursued his man for eight months before finally bringing him to justice. The man arrested at the home of Helen Gould said she had promised to marry him. He was a "lunatic." But, a smart one, if he could evade the entire New York City police force and Bat Masterson for nearly a year.

Much more could be written about Bat Masterson and his law enforcement work, but just like a cat, Bat lived nine lives—continually reinventing himself.

In 1883, Bat Masterson gave up the gun for a much more potent weapon—the pen. The *Dodge City Times* said, "The fine artistic style in which Col. Bat wields the pen is adding fame to his already illustrious name."

And, though he would continue writing for the rest of his life, Bat soon added another notch to his resume—sports promoter.

Boxing, especially, became one of Bat's great passions. In 1888, while refereeing a bout between John P. Clow and Jim Fell, Bat called a questionable foul. Even so, "the crowd received the announcement with shouts of approval," wrote the *Omaha Daily Bee*, "as it was a well-known fact that anyone who questioned any of Masterson's acts never survived a great length of time to talk about it."

In 1893, the *Globe-Republican* speculated Masterson won the Goddard-Smith boxing match in New Orleans. Bat said, "he knew Smith had a yellow streak in him," so he stayed in Smith's corner all night. It was suggested Bat pulled his gun in the ring, telling the boxer, "If you quit, I'll blow your head off." In which case, it was a smoking gun that won the contest, not the pugilist.

Charges of crooked sporting contests would follow Bat for the rest of his life. Then, in 1902, Masterson got arrested for possessing crooked gambling instruments. Also arrested were his partners in crime, James A. Sullivan, J. F. Saunders, and Leopold Frank. Their accuser was a Chicago man named Snow, who said they swindled him out of $17,000 in a game at the Waldorf.

Bat eventually beat the rap and got off with a $10 fine for possessing a firearm.

In 1903, the *Butte Inter Mountain* reported Bat won $30,000 at a faro table in Hot Springs, Arkansas. The paper said, "Masterson is a lucky dog and always was. He could win when nobody else could, and he generally picked the winner in the big prize fights."

In 1904, Bat Masterson visited Teddy Roosevelt at the White House. The two men got along splendidly. Bat visited the President pretty much every day for a week. They talked about old times in the west, ranching, and sporting events—all subjects dear to Roosevelt.

The following year, when the opportunity arose, Roosevelt repaid Bat by pressuring New York Marshal

Hinkel to appoint Bat as a deputy Marshal, a position he held for the next seven years. As a New York marshal, Bat dealt mainly with counterfeiters, moonshiners, and confidence men. He noted that the New York City streets were much more dangerous than any he had ever patrolled in the old west. In New York, every man carried a gun and was dumb enough to use it. When a man didn't want to fight in the old West, he went around unarmed. That way, no one would mess with him. New Yorkers didn't care about honor or fairness. They were quick to shoot and kill.

After leaving the marshal's office in 1912, Bat returned to his writing. He covered sporting events, politics, and local affairs, and sometimes when the spirit moved him, he shared memories of daring times in the old west.

The *Butler Weekly Times* best summarized Bat's troubled life. "His skills with the revolver made him invaluable, and no one ever inquired how many toughs tumbled before his never missing muzzle." For a short time, it required men with nerve and pluck to tame the west. But, as soon as civilization arrived, their usefulness ended.

Bat Masterson died at his writing desk on October 25, 1921. He was 66 years old.

Tom Horn – Cattle Detective

Tom Horn is one of those western characters who's hard to peg. During his short life span, he served as an Indian fighter, deputy sheriff, Pinkerton man, and range detective, but mostly, he worked as a problem solver, offering a final solution for troubled cattlemen.

The *Salt Lake Herald* said, "Horn is alleged to have taken it upon himself to get rid of the rustlers in his own peculiar way and which, he often remarked, was the sure way."

"Doc" Shores, the sheriff of Gunnison County, said Tom Horn "didn't place a high value on human life." As a cattle detective with the Swan Land Cattle Company and the Iron Mountain Ranch Company, Horn earned $600 for the hide of every cattle rustler he brought in. But, Horn told one confidant, I have "no trouble collecting my money, for I would kill a man who cheated me out of ten cents."

Many western writers classify Tom Horn as a gunfighter because he killed at least seventeen men during his days as a range detective. But Tom Horn was no gunfighter. He never faced anyone in a fair fight. Instead, his favorite method of getting his man was to ambush him on the trail or back shoot him from a safe distance—with a Buffalo gun. Tom Horn may have played fast and loose with his victims' lives, but he never took chances with his own.

In his posthumously published autobiography, *The Life of Tom Horn*, Horn claimed to have singlehandedly affected the capture of Geronimo in 1886. "I want to surrender with all my people," Geronimo told him. "I will do as you say and go where you tell me to go or send me. I am tired of the warpath, and my people are all worn out."

From 1886 to 1888, Horn served as a deputy sheriff in Yavapai and Gila County, Arizona. Several years later, he drifted to Denver, Colorado, and "was initiated into the mysteries of the Pinkerton Institution." They hired Horn because of his unique tracking skills. He could sniff out a trail faster than a coon dog trailing a bitch in heat.

Horn said he "never had a very good feeling about the Pinkertons." He thought they spent too much time talking and too little time doing. So when superintendent, James McParland, asked how he would handle a train robbery case, Horn didn't need any time to think about it. He responded, "If I had a good man with me, I could catch up to them."

In August of 1890, Horn got a chance to show the Pinkertons what he had. Someone robbed the Denver and

Rio Grande Railroad at Cotopaxi and Texas Creek. Horn was assigned the case and set out with his assistant, C. W. Shores. After several weeks of tracking, they caught up with Burt Curtis at Washita Station. Shores escorted Curtis back to the Pinkerton office in Denver. Horn stuck around, waiting to round up his accomplice, "Peg Leg" Watson. It didn't take long. "Peg Leg" returned to Washita Station a few weeks later, and Horn captured him singlehandedly.

After that, he tracked Joe McCoy to Ashley, Utah, and arrested him there during Christmas festivities.

Horn said, "I never did like the work [at Pinkerton's], so I left them in 1894." However, the truth was somewhat different. Charlie Siringo, a Pinkerton operative, said the agency separated Horn for committing a robbery in Nevada while he was on their payroll. "William A. Pinkerton told me that Tom Horn was guilty of the crime," said Siringo, "but his people could not allow him to go to prison while in their employ." The implication was Pinkerton covered up Horn's wrongdoings to protect their reputation.

Horn killed two Iron Mountain ranchmen in 1895. William Lewis died while loading beef in his corral. Horn ordered him to throw up his hands, then shot and killed him as he did it. Horn later said Lewis was the most scared man he ever saw. He just rode into his corral and blew him away with his pistol. He gunned down William Powell while he was making hay on his ranch.

In 1896, a ranchman named Campbell disappeared, carrying a large sum of money. Horn was suspected, but there was no body or evidence, so he was never charged in that case.

Soon after that, Horn landed a job as a stock detective with the Swan Land and Cattle Company in Wyoming. His unique services included hunting cattle rustlers and ensuring they didn't rustle cattle anymore. Over time, he performed similar services for the Wyoming Cattleman's Association and the Iron Mountain Cattle Company.

Contemporary accounts credit Horn with sending seventeen rustlers to meet their maker. After he killed his victims, the story is that Horn piled a stack of rocks under his victim's head. It was a sign to his employers he'd started another rustler on the road to hell, and he'd be by soon to collect his due.

Tom Horn served with the 5th Corps in Cuba during the Spanish American War, supervising eight-pack trains. The *New York Times* reported, "Tom Horn will be the boss packer of what will be known as 'Horn's Train.'" Horn "not only superintended the training of the mules but also of the men who served as packers. Only strong men physically are selected, as packing is one of the hardest and most tiresome duties in the army service…The manner in which Tom Horn managed these unruly mules [shows] that gentleness is far better than brutality even in the treatment of a stubborn mule."

As superintendent of the packer corps, Horn didn't participate directly in any battles. However, he was on hand to witness Teddy Roosevelt and the Rougher Riders storming up San Juan Hill.

Within a short time of the war's end, Horn returned to work as a cattle detective. He allegedly shot and killed two cattle rustlers in July of 1900. Matt Rash, of Brown's Park, Colorado, was shot and killed while eating supper in his cabin. Isham Dart died in an ambush near his ranch. The only evidence to tie Horn to the murders was that he was in the vicinity when they occurred.

Horn took his last job in 1901 as a stock detective for John Coble, a wealthy cattle baron. One of his duties was to ensure the sheep of Kels P. Nickell didn't graze on cattle land. Unfortunately, things went bad for Tom Horn on July 10, 1901. Fourteen-year-old Willie Nickell died that day.

Investigators determined Willie Nickell died from two .30-.30 Winchester shots. They said the "assassin was secreted behind a pile of rocks on a little hill overlooking the gate."

At first, the family of James Miller, a neighbor of Nickell's, came under suspicion. Then, the father and his two sons were arrested and questioned because of an ongoing feud with Nickell. Both families had threatened to kill each other.

Eventually, Tom Horn came under suspicion. According to the *Red Lodge Pickett*, the case against Horn rested on two facts: Horn was within two miles of the murder scene just twelve hours before it occurred. And, just four hours after the murder, he rode into Laramie on a "powerful horse which showed the effects of a long, hard ride." Another piece of the puzzle was the murder weapon—a .30-.30 Winchester, Horn's weapon of preference.

Several days later, a man fitting Horn's description left a bundle of clothes at a shoe store in Laramie. A sweater found in the bundle contained human bloodstains. When law enforcement officials showed the sweater to Horn, he admitted it was his.

The most damning evidence came to light a few months after that. Horn drank too much at the Festival of the Mountain and Plain in Denver. Then wagged his tongue a bit too much. Finally, he implied to several of his drinking buddies that he had killed Willie Nickell.

On January 10, 1902, Deputy Marshal Joe Lefors coaxed a confession out of Tom Horn.

Horn told Lefors, "Killing men is my specialty, and I guess I've got a corner on the market in this section." He said he put a stone under his victim's head. The rocks told his employers he did the job.

Horn testified, "I used a .30-.30. I like it better than any other. It carries true to the mark. I thought once the kid would get away from me, but I nailed him. It was the finest shot I ever made and the dirtiest job I ever done."

Horn didn't stop there. He told Lefors he made his first kill when he was twenty-six, a second lieutenant in the Mexican army. He said he got $600 each for killing William Lewis and William Powell. After that, he was paid $500 for killing Willie Nickell.

The *Salt Lake Herald* said Horn admitted to his attorneys "he was lying in wait for Kels Nickell at the time the boy was murdered." Horn said, "He cut the lad off at the gate leading from the Nickell pasture and killed him to prevent him from running to the house and raising a hell of a commotion."

During his trial, Horn said his testimony was a joke. He was drunk and "joshing" with Lefors.

Whatever Horn said, the jury didn't buy it. He was convicted of killing Willie Nickell and sentenced to death by hanging. In a letter written to John Coble moments before he died, Horn said, "I did not kill Willie Nickell. I never made an admission to Lefors, Ohnhaus, or Snow, and all swore to lies, including Irwin of Laramie."

In the end, Tom Horn swung on the gallows for the murder of fourteen-year-old Willie Nickell.

The *Salt Lake Herald* said, "Horn went smiling to [the] scaffold." He "died at 11:08 a.m. game to the last and smiling. He stood with clenched fists waiting for the drop." His friends, Charlie and Frank Irwin, sang, "Keep your hand upon the throttle and your eyes upon the rail" as he walked to the scaffold.

Sixteen minutes later, Tom Horn was pronounced dead. His neck snapped by the hangman's noose.

After Horn's death, William Pinkerton told the *San Francisco Call*, "I doubt whether Tom Horn during his whole life on the frontier ever experienced the sensation of fear."

Heck Thomas - Lawman Extraordinaire

Henry Andrew Thomas, better known as "Heck" Thomas, was in on the kill for some of the west's most dangerous outlaws. He helped take down Bill Dalton, Bill Doolin, and the Lee brothers, a notorious group of Texas cattle rustlers. He rode on the final chase after "Dynamite Dick" Clifton but missed the kill.

Thomas got his start in law enforcement at the age of seventeen when he joined the Atlanta, Georgia, police force. From 1875 to 1885, he worked as a railroad guard for the Texas Express Company. In 1885, he became a member of the Fort Worth Detective Association.

His first big case with them involved tracking down the Lee brothers.

The *Dillon Tribune* said the Lees had been terrorizing Delaware, Bend, and Cook Counties in Texas for nearly two years. They rustled cattle on the Texas side of the Red River and drove them across the river into Indian Territory, where they had ranches. Jim, Bill, and Pink Lee led a gang of twenty cattle thieves in the river country and were said to have killed forty men.

Thomas told the *Dallas Daily Herald* he had been chasing the Lee boys since May 5. "At times, we were in close places and could not tell whether the Lee boys were after us or we after them."

On September 11, Thomas received a tip the Lee brothers were hidden away in the village of Dexter, Texas. He rode out with officers James Taylor and James Settles.

It was raining hard. The posse came upon the gang as they cut the pasture fence on John Washington's ranch. The officers rode up as close as possible, dismounted their horses, and crept up on the suspects.

In his official report, Heck Thomas said, "We got as close to them as possible—about 40 or 45 yards away—and ordered them to surrender. They dropped their nippers and fired at us and missed us; as Pink tried another shell on his gun, he was killed…about a second or two later, Jim was shot by one of us, and about 16 shots were fired; we kept up shooting till Jim quit."

Both brothers died in the fight. When the posse searched the Lees' clothing, they found newspaper clippings detailing their crime spree. Heck Thomas' final comment was, "The fight was in the grass, in the open prairie, and was as pretty a one as I ever saw."

In 1887, Heck got himself shot up while trailing the Purdy Gang. He brought the outlaws in despite taking two bullets and found himself a new wife to boot.

Burrel F. Cox rode with Thomas on that outing. After Heck got shot, Cox, Hank Childers, and Jim Wallace returned fire. They killed Aaron Purdy, the gang leader, and arrested the rest of its members.

Nurse, Matie Mowbray, cared for Thomas' gunshot wounds. After he recovered, they were married.

Heck Thomas and John West captured Oscar Coulter on August 25, 1889. Coulter was a desperate character who first landed in Arkansas at the age of eighteen. In 1880, he got arrested for carrying a pistol in town and threatened revenge against the officer who arrested him.

After his arrest, officers discovered several arrest warrants for Coulter in Georgia. Officer Maysey escorted him there to face charges. Six and a half years later, after his release from prison, Coulter made good on his threat.

On Friday morning, February 27, 1888, he walked into a store in Logan County, Texas, armed with two six-shooters and a Winchester rifle. He pulled his pistol and shot and killed Officer Maysey, now a shopkeeper.

After killing Maysey, Coulter mounted his horse and disappeared into Indian Territory. He robbed a train in Muscogee, Indian Territory, not long after that. When Thomas and West learned his whereabouts, they waited for him along a road they knew he would soon be passing. The *Fort Worth Daily Gazette* reported when the two lawmen confronted Oscar Coulter, "he surrendered and gave us his guns without a murmur."

Thomas became a member of the "Three Guardsmen" in 1891. The other members were Bill Tilghman and Chris Madsen. Together they took down over 300 outlaws and fugitives in the Indian Territory.

After the Adair, Oklahoma train robbery in July 1892, Heck trailed the Dalton Brothers within twenty miles of Coffeyville, Kansas. Before closing in on their campsite, Heck received word of their virtual annihilation during the Coffeyville Bank robbery. He rode into town to help identify the bodies.

One of the "Three Guardsmen's" bigger tests came in 1893. On September 1, Marshal E. D. Nix received a tip that the Doolin-Dalton Gang was hiding in Ingalls, Oklahoma Territory. Ingalls was a small town of roughly 150 people on the dividing line between the Creek Indian Reservation and Oklahoma Territory. It contained two saloons and a house of pleasure with four working girls. The town catered to the outlaws and depended on their wild spending for survival.

The story is the boys were warned about the posse's approach but decided to play out their card game before making their getaway. "Bitter Creek" Newcomb was the first outlaw out the door. He took a bullet from deputy marshal Dick Speed but kept moving.

The rest of the outlaws snuck out a side door. Dan "Dynamite Dick" Clifton and Charlie Pierce took bullets during their escape but eluded the posse.

Bill Doolin killed deputy marshal Dick Speed during the fighting. Bill Dalton shot and killed deputy marshal Lafayette Shadley. "Arkansas Tom" Jones kept the posse pinned down with a deadly fire from his hotel room window. That facilitated the gang's getaway. His gunfire killed deputy marshal Tom Hueston. Unfortunately for Jones, he was captured and sentenced to fifty years in prison.

Heck Thomas and his posse sent Bill Doolin to meet his maker around 2 a.m. on August 25, 1896.

Thomas learned Doolin was spending nights with his wife and two-year-old daughter in a house on the outskirts of Lawson. Doolin would arrive at the house after dark and sneak out before morning. Neighbors knew Doolin was in the area but were afraid to alert law enforcement officials.

When Thomas learned of Doolin's whereabouts, he detailed two men to watch the house.

Captain F. J. Dodge, a special officer with Wells Fargo and Co., said: "it was only by chance that Doolin was caught." Heck Thomas had his posse ready to move in. Doolin left the house about 2 a.m., armed with a

Winchester and a .45 caliber Colt revolver. He started walking towards the posse.

As quick as he heard the posse cry out, "Halt!" Doolin "brought his Winchester to his shoulder and fired two volleys...At almost the same instant, members of the posse fired a volley from their shotguns, and Marshall Thomas discharged his rifle." Doolin took 21 buckshot rounds in the fracas and a "rifle bullet that tore its way through his breast."

In September of 1896, Heck Thomas arrived in Sedalia, Missouri. He was hot on the trail of "Dynamite Dick" Clifton. Clifton had robbed a bank in Southwest City, Missouri, in 1894. Five of the seven robbers were killed in a running fight with officers and townspeople that day. "Dynamite Dick" and another gang member escaped to Indian Territory.

Thomas received word "Dynamite Dick" was hiding in a farmhouse near Clifton City. Unfortunately for Thomas, "Dynamite Dick" was tipped off about the posse and escaped just ahead of them.

It was a short reprieve. "Dynamite Dick" was killed in 1897. After months of searching, deputy marshal George Lawson and Hess Bussey tracked "Dynamite Dick" to a cabin outside of Checotah, Indian Territory. When challenged by the posse to throw down his guns, "Dynamite Dick" burst through the door—a six-shooter in both hands—blasting at the marshals. Seconds later, "Dynamite Dick" fell dead.

On October 14, 1896, Heck Thomas and his posse took down the Green Gang in a shootout at Dologsh, Indian Territory.

The *Daily Ardmoreite* said the Green Gang had been terrorizing the area for nearly two years. The posse surrounded the gang as they attempted to rob a nearby store. The paper said, "It is said that the dead bodies of the two desperadoes were seen lying on the depot platform at Dologsh, where they had been shot down by Deputy Marshal Heck Thomas and posse."

In 1902, Thomas became the police chief of Lawton, Oklahoma.

Life in Lawton proved uneventful for Thomas, who'd spent most of his life riding the range and taking down high-profile criminals. 1904 brought a breath of excitement to the town. The *Butler Weekly Times* reported, "Bullets fly thick on Lawton Street." L. T. Russell, the former editor of the *Daily Democrat*, shot down J. W. Hawkins, the former assistant chief of police. The two men had been engaged in a long-time feud. On the day of the shooting, Hawkins pushed Russell down. As he was falling, Russell pulled his revolver and began firing. Hawkins took three bullets—one in the upper leg, one in the knee, and one in the abdomen.

He was taken to Heck Thomas' house and died less than a week later from his wounds.

The *Chickasha Daily Express* printed an interesting anecdote about Thomas in 1906. Thomas was fishing on Medicine Creek in his custom seersucker suit. One thing led to another, and he fell into the drink. He quickly got out, but the fabric began to shrink as the day went on, and Thomas got stuck in his suit. They said, "the pants took the cake. They shrunk until they fit him as tight as the skin of a sausage...When he arrived home, he said he had to use a bootjack to pull off his pants."

Heck Thomas retired from police work in 1907. He died of Bright's disease in August 1912.

Bill Tilghman – Frontier Lawman, Politician, and Movie Maker

Bill Tilghman got his start as a buffalo hunter in the early 1870s. Along with his partner, George Rust, Tilghman signed on with the Atchison, Topeka, and Santa Fe Railroad in 1872—promising to bring in 50 buffalo a week to feed their construction crews. By the time Tilghman left the line in 1875, the two men had taken down close to 12,000 buffalo.

After that, Tilghman tried his luck at a string of jobs—ranching, running a saloon in Dodge City, Kansas, and serving as a deputy for Bat Masterson in Ford County, Kansas. Not long after that, there was some talk that Bill participated in a train robbery and stole some horses—but none of it stuck. From 1883 to 1886, Tilghman served as a deputy for Pat Sughrue in Dodge City.

In 1889, at the start of the Oklahoma land boom, he staked a claim near Guthrie, Oklahoma, and took up ranching. A few years later, in 1893, Tilghman was appointed city marshal of Perry, Oklahoma. Heck Thomas was his assistant marshal. Together, they proceeded to clean up the town.

The *Wichita Daily Eagle* ran a story about Tilghman that year. They described him as "tall and slim, straight as an arrow, and is not afraid of anything living. He never gets excited, talks but little, and in the performance of his duties, does not seem to know the meaning of the word failure." The implication was that once he started a case, Tilghman would not give up until he got his man.

His wife, Zoe Tilghman, published an article in *Life Magazine* on May 18, 1959. She said the movies gave a false impression of western lawmen. They "hated to kill and never boasted about it." It was just something they needed to do to clean up the frontier to make it safe for families to move in.

In 1894 and 1895, two teenage girls caused a stir in Indian Territory—peddling whisky and stealing horses. Jennie "Little Britches" Stevens and "Cattle Annie" McDougal were just sixteen and thirteen when they were accused of running messages for the Doolin-Dalton gang.

Tilghman, and another lawman, Steve Burke, chased the girls down to a farmhouse outside Pawnee, Oklahoma. When they moved in on them, the girls took off on horseback. Steve Burke rode off after "Cattle Annie." Tilghman chased after "Little Britches."

Even though she was only sixteen, "Little Britches" challenged Bill's man-hunting skills. While he was chasing after her, "Little Britches" turned and let loose with her Winchester, sending a bevy of hot lead swirling around the marshal's head. Tilghman pulled back to regroup, then charged the girl, shot down her horse, tackled her, and brought her to the ground. Tilghman took some scratches and bites when it was all said and done.

On July 6, 1895, "Cattle Annie" was sentenced to one year in Federal prison for peddling whisky to the Osage Indians. "Little Britches" was sentenced to two years for horse theft and whisky peddling.

In September of 1895, Bill Tilghman found himself hot on the trail of Bill Raidler, a member of the Doolin-Dalton gang. The *Wichita Daily Eagle* wrote, "The officer and the outlaw came together in the brush, in the Triangle country. They opened on each other at the same time but shot from Tilghman's gun clipped the middle finger of the outlaw's right, or pistol hand, and he turned his horse around, first biting off the mangled finger and spitting it at his opponent, and rode away."

Tilghman was confident he knew where Raidler was hiding out. He waited all night outside a log cabin, armed with a double-barreled shotgun loaded with buckshot. Raidler came out about sunrise. Tilghman hollered for him to "throw up his hands." Instead, Raidler went for his gun.

Tilghman let loose with both barrels of his shotgun. Raidler fell after taking several buckshot to his head and arm.

Later at his trial, the *San Francisco Call* reported, "the defense practically admitted that Raidler had participated in the [Dover] train robbery." But his defense said he shouldn't be found guilty because the mailbags weren't touched. Nevertheless, Raidler received a ten-year sentence and was later released in 1903. He was one of only two members of the Doolin-Dalton gang to survive into the new century. The other was Roy Dougherty. In 1915, he did a short stint as an actor, then returned to the outlaw life, robbing a bank in Neosho, Missouri, in 1917. He died seven years later, in 1924, at 54.

Tilghman arrested Bill Doolin single-handedly on January 18, 1896. The lawman had been on Doolin's trail for a year, on and off, when he tracked him to a farm near Burden, Kansas. Doolin had been living there for some four months, going under the alias of Thomas Wilson. After a short investigation, Tilghman discovered Doolin drove an old lumber wagon into town every two weeks to get supplies. Six weeks into his stakeout, there was no sign of Doolin, and it appeared as if he had made a clean getaway.

Tilghman said he wasn't sure why, but he had an idea he'd find Doolin in Eureka Springs. He went there purely on a hunch. As soon as he arrived in town, Tilghman saw Bill Doolin walk into the Davy House hotel.

Tilghman decided to get a haircut first before pursuing his man. "To his surprise, Doolin was sitting there reading a paper, but he did not recognize him. The marshal slipped into the bathroom and, reappearing, quickly covered the outlaw with his revolver." Doolin made a move for his gun, thought the better of it, and threw his hands up. Tilghman had the barbershop owner disarm Doolin while he kept him undercover.

Bill Doolin later told the *Wichita Daily Eagle*, "When he [Tilghman] came into the barbershop, I thought I had seen him somewhere, but he brushed by me so fast and called for a bath in such an unconcerned way that I just went on reading my paper. The next I knew, he was standing four feet from me, and I was looking straight into his gun." Doolin said he knew Tilghman had the "nerve" and would kill him if necessary. "If it had been anybody else, I would not have hesitated to pull my gun."

Because his captor was Bill Tilghman, Doolin surrendered without a fight and allowed Tilghman to take him in. When they arrived at the Santa Fe Depot in Guthrie, Oklahoma, a crowd of nearly 2,000 people gathered around, waiting to catch a glimpse of the sandy-haired outlaw.

Tilghman became the sheriff of Lincoln County, Oklahoma, in 1899. Five years later, he was a member of the Oklahoma delegation of the Democratic National

Convention in St. Louis. Tilghman became an Oklahoma State Senator in 1910 and chief of police in Oklahoma City in 1911.

In 1915, Tilghman's career took a 360-degree turn. He produced and acted in a silent movie called *Passing of the Oklahoma Outlaws*. It was set in the Indian Territory, in the actual locations where many of the scenes originally took place. Where possible, he also had many of the original characters re-enact their life stories.

Tilghman made the movie because he was concerned about how Hollywood portrayed outlaws as heroes and lawmen as a bunch of bumbling boobs. The film was wildly successful during its day and played all over the country.

For most people, that would have ended a highly successful career in law enforcement, politics, and film. But, for Bill Tilghman, it launched his re-entry into police work. In 1924, at 72, he became marshal of the boomtown of Cromwell, Oklahoma. Then, on November 21 of that year, he was shot dead by an off-duty U. S. Prohibitions agent named Wiley Lynn.

There are two stories about how he died.

The most likely story says that Wiley Lynn pulled up in front of Pop Murphy's dance hall and began shooting his gun off. Tilghman went to arrest him, and Wiley shot him three times.

The other version of the story says Tilghman was protecting the saloon keepers. When Wiley Lynn tried to raid Pop Murphy's dance hall to shut them down for selling liquor, Tilghman told him he'd kill him if he tried. Wiley was the first to grab his gun and shoot Tilghman dead.

Knowing Tilghman's reputation, the first version seems more likely.

Appendix 1: Gunfight at the O. K. Corral

*(This is one of the first reports of the gunfight at the O. K. Corral. It was printed in the **Arizona Weekly Citizen** on October 30, 1881, and is reprinted here. So for anyone looking for a first-hand report of the famous gun battle, this is as good as it gets.)*

A Desperate Street Fight

Marshal Virgil Earp, Morgan and Wyatt Earp, and Doc Holliday meet the cowboys—Three men killed and two wounded, one seriously—Origin of the trouble and its tragical termination.

(Tombstone Nugget (October 27)

The 26th of October will always be marked as one of the crimson days in the annals of Tombstone, a day when blood flowed as water. Human life was held as shuttlecock, a day always to be remembered as witnessing the bloodiest and deadliest street fight that has ever occurred in this place, or probably in the territory.

The origin of the trouble dates back to the first arrest of Stillwell and Spencer for the robbery of the Bisbee stage. The co-operation of the Earps with the sheriff and his deputies in the arrest causing a number of the cowboys, too, it is said, to threaten the lives of all interested in the capture. Still, nothing occurred to indicate that any such threats would be carried into execution. But Tuesday night Ike Clanton and Doc Holliday had some difficulty in the Alhambra saloon. Hard words passed between them, and when they parted, it was generally understood that the feeling between the two men was that of intense hatred.

Yesterday morning Clanton came on the street armed with a rifle and revolver but was almost immediately arrested by Marshal Earp, disarmed, and fined by Justice Wallace for carrying concealed weapons. While in the courtroom, Wyatt Earp told him that as he had made threats against his life, he wanted him to make his fight, to say how, when and where he would fight, and to get his crowd, and he (Wyatt) would be on hand.

In reply, Clanton said: "Four feet of ground is enough for me to fight on, and I'll be there." A short time after this, William Clanton and Frank McLowry came in town, and as Thomas McLowry was already here, the feeling soon became general that a fight would ensue before the day was over, and crowds of expectant men stood on the corner of Allen and Fourth streets awaiting the coming conflict. It was now about two o'clock, and at this time, Sheriff Behan appeared upon the scene and told Marshal Earp that if he disarmed his posse, composed of Morgan and Wyatt Earp, and Doc Holliday, he would go down to the O. K. Corral where Ike and James Clanton and Frank and Tom Lowry were and disarm them. The Marshal did not desire to do this until assured that there was no danger of attack from the other party. The sheriff went to the corral and told the cowboys to put their arms away and not make any trouble. Ike Clanton and Tom McLowry said they were not armed, and Frank McLowry said he would not lay his aside. In the meantime, the Marshal had concluded to go and, if possible, end the matter by disarming them, and as he and his posse came down Fremont Street towards the corral, the sheriff stepped out and said: "Hold up, boys. Don't go down there, or there will be trouble; I have been down there to disarm them."

But they passed on, and when within a few feet of them, the marshal said to the Clantons and McLowrys: "Throw up your hands, boys. I intend to disarm you." As he spoke, Frank McLowry made a motion to draw his revolver when Wyatt Earp pulled his and shot him, the ball striking on the right side of his abdomen. About the same time, Doc Holliday shot Tom McLowry in the right side, using a short shotgun, such as is carried by Wells, Fargo, and Co's messengers. In the meantime, Billy Clanton had shot at

Morgan Earp, the ball passing through the point of the left shoulder blade across his back, just grazing the backbone and coming out at the shoulder, the ball remaining inside of his shirt. He fell to the ground but, in an instant, gathered himself and, raising in a sitting position, fired at Frank McLowry as he crossed Fremont Street, and at the same instant, Doc Holliday shot at him, both balls taking effect, either of which would have proved fatal, as one struck him in the right temple and the other in the left breast. As he started across the street, however, he pulled his gun down on Holliday, saying, "Blaze away! You're a daisy if you have," replied Doc. This shot of McLowry's passed through Holliday's pistol pocket, just grazing the skin.

While this was going on, Billy Clanton had shot Virgil Earp in the right leg, the ball passing through the calf, inflicting a severe flesh wound. In turn, he had been shot by Morgan Earp in the right side of the abdomen and twice by Virgil Earp, once in the right wrist and once in the left breast. Soon after the shooting commenced, Ike Clanton ran through the O. K. Corral, across Allen Street into Kellogg's saloon, and thence into Toughnut Street, where he was arrested and taken to the county jail. The firing altogether didn't occupy more than twenty-five seconds, during which time fully thirty shots were fired. After the fight was over, Billy Clanton, who, with wonderful vitality, survived his wounds for fully an hour, was carried by the editor and foreman of the *Nugget* into a house near where he lay, and everything possible done to make his last moments easy. He was game to the last, never uttering a word of complaint, and just before his last, he said, "Goodbye, boys; go away and let me die." The wounded were taken to their houses and, at three o'clock this morning, were resting comfortably. The dead bodies were taken in charge by the coroner, and an inquest will be held upon them at ten o'clock today. Upon the person of Thomas McLowry was found between $300 and $400, and checks and certificates of deposit to the amount of nearly $3000.

During the shootings, Sheriff Behan was standing nearby, commanding the contestants to cease firing but was powerless to prevent it. Several parties who were in the vicinity of the shooting had narrow escapes from being shot. One man who had lately arrived from the East had a ball pass through his pants. He left for home this morning. A person called "the Kid," who shot Hicks at Charleston recently was also grazed by a ball. When the Vizina whistle gave the signal that there was a conflict between the officers and the cowboys, the mines on the hill shut down, and the miners were brought to the surface. From the Contention Mine, a number of men, fully armed, were sent to town in a four-horse carriage. At the request of the sheriff, the "vigilantes" or Committee of Safety were called from the streets by a few sharp toots of the Vizina whistle. During the early part of the evening, there was a rumor that a mob would attempt to take Ike Clanton from the jail and lynch him, and to prevent any such unlawful proceedings, a strong guard of deputies was placed around that building and will be so continued until all danger is past. At 8 o'clock last evening, Finn Clanton, a brother of Billy and Ike, came in town and, placing himself under the guard of the sheriff, visited the morgue to see the remains of one brother and then passed the night in jail in company with the other.

Ominous sounds. Shortly after the shooting ceased, the whistle at the Vizina Mine sounded a few short toots, and almost simultaneously, a large number of citizens appeared on the streets, armed with rifles and a belt of cartridges around their waists. These men formed in line and offered their services to the peace officers to preserve order in case any attempt at disturbance was made or any interference was provided to the officers of the law. However, no hostile move was offered by anyone, and quiet and order was fully restored, and in a short time, the excitement died away.

At the morgue. The bodies of the three slain cowboys lay side by side, covered with a sheet. Very little blood appeared on their clothing, and only on the face of young

Billy Clanton was there any distortion of the features or evidence of pain in dying. The features of the two McLowry boys looked as calm and placid in death as if they had died peaceably, surrounded by loving friends and sorrowing relatives. No unkind remarks were made by anyone, but a feeling of unusual sorrow seemed to prevail at the sad occurrence. Of the McLowry brothers, we could learn nothing of their previous history before coming to Arizona. The two brothers owned quite an extensive ranch on the San Pedro, some seventy or eighty miles from this city, to which they had removed their band of cattle since the recent Mexican and Indian troubles. They did not beat the reputation of being of a quarrelsome disposition but were known as fighting men and have gener[ally]conducted themselves in a quiet and orderly manner when in Tombstone.

Appendix 2: Methods of Gunfighters

(Interesting article on methods of the gunfighters first published in *The Salt Lake Herald*, December 29, 1889.)

Pistol Practice
Some Odd Ways of Firing
Rapidly Explained

A writer in *The San Francisco Examiner* gives the true story of the shooting iron in the far west. There have come many remarkable yarns as to the way "quick work" is done in the land of the cowboys' gun, but in the article mentioned, the writer gets down to hard facts and specialties. He avers that the western gunner strips his revolver of all superfluities and leaves nothing to keep it from being discharged but his own thumb. The "gunfighter," says the writer, "who permits the gun maker to prescribe the manner of using a gun is not extant he is dead." The live gunfighter is he who spoiled his weapon as soon as he bought it by removing the trigger and reducing the working parts of the lock to hammer mainspring and cylinder pawl.

This has been brought about by that quickness which is essential among people who don't trouble the law to take care of them but do it all themselves. The question often arises between two men, "Which of us is to die?" The matter is settled by the time taken by each to lodge bullets in the other person. Scientists have measured "personal equation," which is the time taken for the brain to convey an order through the nerves to the muscles and for the muscles to execute the order. Perhaps the western cowboy will soon bring his firing down to so fine a point that his personal equation will settle the matter. Then he need only send to some college professor to measure it and the other fellow to know whether to arrange his affairs for departure from the world.

When the self-cocker came out, it bid fair to be immensely popular. About this, the aforesaid writer says:

"The makers of pistols thought they had produced a perfect weapon—one that met all the demands gentlemen in the killing line—when they devised a double-action revolver, and for a short time, the self-cocker had a great tale on the frontier. A few years ago, no Texas cowboy or ranger, no Colorado sheriff, Arizona rustler, or Panhandle tough considered himself correctly dressed unless he had a double-action frontier six-shooter or two at his belt.

"But time developed the imperfections and shortcoming of the self-cocker. Theoretically, it seemed perfect, but in actual use, it developed a dangerous tendency to get out of kilter. Its mechanism was too complicated and delicate. After a little wear of the lock, when a gentleman desired to assassinate an acquaintance, he was likely to be disappointed by the failure of the trigger to carry the hammer back to the proper notch, or perhaps the cylinder would forget to revolve, and the acquaintance would have time to insert a knife into his stomach or cave in his head with a club, which was very unsatisfactory. Thus the self-cocker incurred the deep displeasure of the fighting men.

"They jeered at its eccentricities, abused it for its little weaknesses, and discarded it from their toilet. The windows of pawnshops and second-hand gun stores were filled with large, dangerous-looking double-action revolvers, which thereby were made familiar to the eastern tourist and the globe trotter. The faster the cowboy and the sheriff threw away these guns, the more firmly fixed became the belief in the lay mind, so to speak, that the self-cocker was the favorite weapon of the frontier because that style of gun was most frequently seen in the dealers' windows. While the western gunfighter was ordering plain, single-action revolvers, the makers were diligently unloading their stock of complicated self-cockers on the tenderfoot."

But where life depends on a fraction of a second, the man whose life is at stake will naturally be hunting for some way of stealing a march on his antagonist. Someone interested improved upon the maker's method in the single-action pistol by what is called "fanning the hammer." This is holding the weapon firmly gripped, with the forearm pressed against the side of the body for steadiness and keeping the trigger back against the guard with the forefinger so that it never engages with the hammer, and rapidly striking the thumb-ear of the hammer with the edge of the left palm. This discharges several shots in quick succession. The trick was first introduced in New Mexico. Extravagant yarns have been told about the unerring precision with which the cowboy will shoot by "fanning the hammer," but these stories are exaggerated. The trick does quick work but not accurate work.

"In 1881, a cowboy named Bob Sinclair worked this new trick in Albuquerque. For some reason or other, he had concluded that Jack Riley was an improper person and that the continued existence of Mr. Riley was an impertinence not to be tolerated. Wherefore he fanned the hammer at Riley. There is no doubt that Mr. Sinclair made a great deal of noise in a very short time. His performance on the six-shooter was rhythmic and inspiring, and the sweep of his left hand was a poem. A carpenter shingling the roof of the new hotel received one bullet in his right heel; some glassware behind the bar of the corner saloon was broken; an Indian card party behind a lumber pile two blocks up the street was dispersed with the loss of one back; a fourth ball inserted itself in Mr. Sinclair's left foot, and the other two escaped in the confusion and are still at large. After the smoke of battle had cleared way, Mr. Riley picked up a board and swatted Mr. Sinclair on the ear."

It is not claimed that this is the "Mr. Riley they spoke of so highly," but he deserves all the encomiums any one of the name ever received.

"When the novelty had worn off this trick," the writer goes on, "the men who carried guns for business purposes and had a serious aim in life, viz., the shortening of it for other people—the men who were not enamored of mere noise and pistol pyrotechnics—took the triggers out of their guns or lashed them firmly back against the guards, thereby throwing them out of commission. The adoption of the triggerless gun made necessary the acquirement of skill in new method of handling the weapon.

The first and most obvious scheme was to work the hammer with the thumb in the ordinary way, letting the hammer slip and fall when the aim was secured. Anybody who tries this for first time will discover that it is not easy to shoot where he looks or to hold the weapon steady. In quick-firing, the pistol is raised and carried back over the shoulder and then thrown sharply forward and downward.

The thumb, grasping the hammer, cocks it during the downward movement, and when the barrel is at the desired position, the hammer is released, and the weapon discharged.

"A revolver can be fired very rapidly in this manner, but no great accuracy of aim can be obtained. A novice would find it difficult to hit a door at twenty feet, and an expert is doing pretty well to hit within the outlines of a man at ten paces. The cowboy who can hit an oyster can at ten feet, throwing the pistol down in the manner described, is a rare bird."

This is the trick that a famous scoundrel called "Curly Bill" practiced on a sheriff in Tombstone. Bill, being ordered by Sheriff White to give up his weapons, took a self-cocker from his belt and handed it toward the sheriff, butt foremost. Just as the sheriff, thrown off his guard, reached for the weapon, Bill whirled it over in his hand, pulled the trigger, and murdered the officer.

The same trick can be done with a triggerless revolver. The weapon is laid in the palm of the hand, butt to the front and right. The forefinger, slipped through the guard, serves as a pivot upon which the pistol turns when given a quick twirl, the other fingers assisting in giving the weapon impetus and grasping the butt when it comes into position. Just before the revolver comes down to a level, the thumb catches and retains the hammer long enough to draw it back. The thumb is then allowed to slip from the hammer, and bang goes the gun. It will be found that a very sharp and sudden movement is required to perform this feat, and the heavier the pistol, the more readily it can be done. It is useless to try it with the pocket toys usually carried.

The joyous jugglers with pistols who keep the ammunition factories going have devised some variations of Curly Bills great play, all of them interesting as tricks but about as useful in border warfare as jig steps in a walking match. For example, the pistol is held as though to be surrendered, lying in the palm of the right hand, the second finger hooked over the hammer. A sharp twirl throws the barrel down and outward, and the forearm is brought up. The second finger simultaneously pulls the hammer back, and the action of closing the finger around the butt releases the hammer. In the performance of this trick, the strength of the middle finger is the principal factor. To do it well, a man must have very strong hands, and he will get many a blister before he succeeds in the trick. If he begins with a loaded weapon, probably his first achievement will be filling his own stomach with lead.

A better variation is achieved by using the thumb to cock the weapon. The revolver rests in the palm in a very innocent-looking position, butt to the left and hammer under the thumb. By sharply closing the hand and giving the weapon a whirl downward, the hammer is drawn back to full cock, and the barrel brought to a level wrong side up. As the thumb slips over the hammer to grasp the butt, the revolver is discharged, and the other man gets hit if he happens to be in the way.

It is possible to imagine circumstances under which adroitness in juggling with pistols might be useful, but it is one chance in a million that a man ever will get caught in such a fix or have an opportunity to work such schemes. A traveler might get away with a stupid road agent by an underhand shot, but ordinarily, the man who wants another's revolver is smart enough to keep the drop and take the weapon from holster or pocket with his own disengaged hand.

The common cowboy of commerce, who is notoriously a marvelous pistol shot but actually a very mediocre marksman and a regular duffer with a gun, delights in tricks and juggling. He can twirl his pistol in the air and bang away at the wide, wide world with great satisfaction to himself and danger to the spectators, but he can't do one-tenth of the things that he brags about doing. In plain, straightaway, efficient shooting, he is no match for any one of half a dozen citizens of San Francisco. Anybody who tells about seeing frontiersmen shoot dimes in the air, perforate distant oyster cans with countless bullets while riding at full speed, drive nails off hand and without taking careful sight, and all the other popularly accepted marvels talks blue bosh. The man who could do such things with a revolver could make more money in a month by giving public exhibitions than he can get punching cows for five years.

The revolver is of use on the frontier in killing men who are unpopular or otherwise objectionable, and the man who can draw quickly and hit a man across the street is a good enough shot for all practical purposes. Mr. Neagle, who is considered a pretty handyman with a pocket gun, held his weapon in both hands when he shot Mr. Terry, who stood within two or three feet of him, and even then, he missed with one bullet.

Appendix 3: Four Bad Men Who Made a Specialty of Carrying Guns

(This article on four western gunfighters—Bat Masterson, Doc Holliday, Luke Short, and Wyatt Earp was published in the *Omaha Daily Bee* on March 13, 1887. It offers an interesting look at their life and times.)

An El Paso (Tex.) correspondent says: When Luke Short, a bad man with a record, shot Jim Courtwright, another bad man with a record, at Fort Worth recently, he reduced the professional killers of the west to a quartet. The list stands at present, in order of precedence, Bat Masterson, Doc Holliday, Luke Short, and Wyatt Earp. There used to be more, but the same wise providence that disintegrated the Jesse James gang and distributed it among the cemeteries, penitentiaries, and dime museums of the land, has elected that bad men eventually kill each other. Thus the supply has been kept ahead of the demand. The interest that attaches to those men is purely transitory; a dead killer is as quickly forgotten as a knocked-out pugilist, but the qualities of nerve and desperation that brought them to the surface in a country where everybody carries a "gun" and people go to glory every day without a benediction or a bootjack stamps them as rather extraordinary characters. Bat Masterson first became a border celebrity through this paper, in which a correspondent rehearsed his pedigree some years ago. Since that time, more has been written about him than all the other three put together. He is the Maud S. of man killers. Nobody has ever lowered his record, but he claims that the twenty-six or twenty-seven inmates of his private graveyard were all sent thither in pursuit of his duty as an officer.

All his life has been spent on the frontier. He was first a cowboy, then a scout in the United States employ, and afterward marshal in several western towns, notably Dodge City, Kansas, and Trinidad, Colorado. Personally, Masterson is the best extant specimen of the gentleman desperado, copyrighted by Bret Harte. He has trained the voice that erstwhile yelled for cows down to a low, gentle baritone; he always dresses in black, wears no jewelry save a slender gold thread of a watch chain; a white cambtic handkerchief peeps from the breast pocket of his four-button cutaway, and he is careful about his boots and ties. A friend who invaded his room when he was here recently found two six-shooters and a manicure set on his bureau. He never blusters. When he gets mad, his mustache creeps up under his nose in a peculiar smile that has no merriment in it, and he reaches for his revolver, which he carries thrust in the waistband of his "pants," directly under the lower buttons of his vest. It looks like the irony of fate that such a man should gravitate into a theatrical husband. Such, however, was the destiny of Masterson. Not long since, he married Nellie McMahon, a western soubrette; and now he carries the pug and wears fur on his overcoat collar. Mrs. Masterson (nee McMahon) is not troubled with mashers.

Doc Holliday was a dentist at Tombstone, Arizona before he became a killer. When he gave up the forceps for the six-shooter, his old patients said it was simply a change of method. The glare of publicity first struck him in 1883 in an article in *Harper's Monthly*, descriptive of a trip through the territories and detailing, in connection, a street tragedy at Tombstone. At the time, a deadly feud existed there between the gambling fraternity and the cowboys. When killings were a matter of almost daily occurrence, a long, lean man with a straw-colored mustache and a facile six-shooter suddenly bloomed out as a leader of the sports. This was Doc Holliday. He killed three or four cowboys, and his careless indifference to danger made him conspicuous even among his daredevil associates. He did not know what fear was, and when the town became too hot to hold him, calmly walked out, down the length of the main street, through a continuous cross-fire from both sides. But the friends and relatives of his victims were relentless. Warrants were sworn out, and he fled to Durango, Col. The leading men of that place feared his presence might discourage immigration and determined to get rid of him. Accordingly, one night at 12, Holliday was awakened by the deep-tolling of the boil that called the Vigilante Committee together.

He knew that a lynching was on foot, realized that he would probably furnish the subject, and quietly jumped out of a back window. Everything grew still, and he was slipping out of town when at the end of the street, he saw the motionless figure of a man on horseback barring the way. The horseman sat his saddle like a statue of bronze, and the fugitive marked the dusky barrel of a Winchester balanced across the bow. Every road had been guarded in advance. Holliday treaded his way back, keeping in the shadows. He felt the circle of pursuit closing on him. His haunts were being ransacked; the sound of opening and shutting doors came to him on the night air and then the tramp of men. It came nearer and nearer when of a sudden, his eyes fell upon a wooden gutter crossing almost at his feet. In an instant, he had crawled underneath, and a moment later and his pursuers passed over where he lay. He stayed there all that night, the next day, and the following night walked over a mountain pass toward Leadville, where society was less exclusive. An effort was made to get him back to

Arizona, but the governor of Colorado refused to sign the requisition papers, and he has since lived at Leadville and Denver. He was at Colorado Springs for a while, but was not regarded as a suitable accessory to a health resort, and got the hint to leave. He ekes out a livelihood as a faro dealer and "stake player."

Luke Short illustrates the fact that a bad man (the term is used in its conventional sense) can acquire a reputation without "killing a great many men. Jim Courtwright was only his second. Something about his manner, difficult to describe—for he is by no means a braggart—convinced people that he was a good man to let alone. He was always cool and imperturbable. The first man he killed was Charley Storms, a gambler. Storms began shooting at him from across the street, and Short, quietly dropping on one knee, aimed over his elbow and sent a bullet through his heart.

Luke Short is a gambler by profession. He is very small, about five feet four inches tall, and weighs somewhere near 140 pounds—without his gun. He obtained national notoriety some years ago through being exiled by the authorities of Dodge City and returning with all the noted desperadoes of the west to claim his own. Such a collection of bad men was never seen in one spot before. They all made their headquarters at the "Long Branch," Short's saloon, and promenaded the streets in a body, armed to the teeth. The expense of purchasing clothes, food, and whisky for his congress of killers eventually forced Short to leave Dodge, and he went to Fort Worth, Texas, where he became interested in a rather gorgeous saloon called the White Elephant. He is the most popular man of his class and, when not professionally engaged, is really disposed to be quiet and pleasant in his manners. Oddly enough, he is a well-posted biblical student and fond of arguing on religious topics.

An incident will illustrate the fearlessness of this man occurred at Salida, Col., in 1881. A foot race been arranged between a couple of local sprinters. Short-backed one and had fixed things to win by what is technically known as a "double-cross." That is to say, his man agreed to sell out to the other side to lose the race but had it privately understood with Short to win anyhow. The referee got a tip and promised to see the thing through. On the day of the race, the track was lined with the toughest kind of western sports, and upwards of $8,000 was bet on the result. All, however, did not come out according to program, for, as is customary with sprinters, the crooked racer decided to double-cross Short himself and actually did lose the race by about four feet. Amid tremendous excitement, the referee, stakeholder, and winners adjourned to a neighboring saloon to divide the spoils, but before the money was produced, Short strode in, his hand on his pistol, and inquired:

"Who won that race?"

"Why didn't you see?" asked the referee.

"Who won that race?" repeated Short.

"I guess your man won it by about a foot," replied the referee, getting out of range.

"I thought so," said Short, coolly taking the sheaf of bills out of the nerveless hand of the stakeholder. "The fact is, gentlemen," he continued as he moved toward the door, "you know my man can win, but you did your best to rob me, and I just reversed things on you." By next to a miracle, he got away with the money. The following day John Cozad, the referee, was poisoned by unknown parties.

Jim Courtwright, the man Short killed, was a tall, rawboned individual with a suspicious stare and a thin, sallow face. He was the sort of a man who is almost inseparably connected on the frontier with an official star; in fact, he was a life-long officer, having been a sheriff, marshal, detective, and agent of the department of justice, United States. His record as a killer was a long and gory one but included a number of Mexicans and Indians, whom the border authorities do not count, but threw out of the returns. During the late great southwestern railroad strike, he added a couple of homicides to his tally, and at the time of his death, the New Mexican authorities were trying to get him to try for murder. Nobody realized better the danger of having a record, and he always carried two heavy revolvers. Noblesse oblige. A bad man may be called on at any moment to defend the title. Short's defense was that Courtwright reached for his revolver, and to allow him to pull it was death. So it seems that every sort of greatness has its drawbacks.

Wyatt Earp, the last of the quartet, was evolved from the license, liberty, turmoil, danger, and outlaw that he always fringed the ragged edge of civilization with red tire.

He came to the front easily and naturally and has many of the qualities of a leader about him. He was the cause of numerous tragedies, but it can be truthfully said that his presence checked a good many more, for he was an officer when his killing took place. His record was made in Arizona at about the time Doc Holliday distinguished himself there, and since that time, he has lived in that territory, Texas and New Mexico. Personally, Earp is tall and slim. He has red hair and wears one of those long, drooping moustache in which a section of the beard is worked in to bring it to the edge of the jaw. He is the last of three brothers, territorial vendetta having disposed of the others.

Of late years Earp has been a gambler. His last exploit in that line was at Tombstone, Ariz., where he turned up with a Chicago sport named Hamilton and a couple of companions and shortly after began playing faro with phenomenal success. The party won so much and so regularly that it was soon apparent that they had some sort of an advantage over the game, but what it was, nobody was able to discover. They nearly broke up the gambling at Tombstone, and the games were finally barred to them. It subsequently leaked out that the edges of the cards had been marked and were read by means of a convened mirror attached to the sleeve of a man who sat next to the dealing box. He guided the other by his bets, and as he only played a few chips at a time, he was not suspected. To those who understand the cheerful game, this explanation will be reasonably clear. Since this episode, Earp has not figured much on the surface.

Appendix 4: First Account of Coffeyville, Kansas Bank Raid by the Dalton Brothers

(This was one of the first published accounts of the Coffeyville, Kansas, bank raid that **wiped out** the Dalton gang. It's a well-written account of what happened that day and contains a list of those citizens and outlaws killed. It was published in *The Wichita Daily Eagle* on October 6th, 1892—the day after the robbery.)

THE NOTORIOUS DALTON BANDITS SHOT TO DEATH

An Attempt to rob the banks of Coffeyville Results in a Bloody Battle in the Streets.

Five of the robbers sent to their last account, and an equal number of the citizens slain. Bob Dalton, the Leader of the gang, falls at the first fire, and his two brothers share his fate. But One survivor of the band of six succeeds in getting out of town, with a posse in hot pursuit.

Coffeyville, Kans. Oct. 5. Bob and Grat Dalton, Thomas Evans, and Jack Moore, all members of the Dalton gang, were killed in this city this morning, and Emmett Dalton lies here mortally wounded. Four of our citizens City Marshal Charles T. Connelly, Charles Brown, George Cubine, and Lucius Baldwin, have also joined the silent majority, sent there by bullets from the robbers' guns, while Cashier Thomas G. Ayers lies at the point of death from a Winchester ball, which struck him in the groin. This is the result of an attempt of the Dalton gang to rob both the banks of this city this morning at 9:45 o'clock.

The robbers succeeded in entering C. M. Condon & Co.'s and the First National bank and securing some twenty-three thousand dollars, but here they got a block away from the scene, four of them bit the dust. The fifth was found nearly a mile out of town. Accounts differ, but it is thought that six men composed the party, consisting of Bob, Grat and Emmett Dalton, Tom Evans, Jack Moore, and Allie Ogee. If the latter was in the party, he alone escaped. Bob and Emmett worked the First National Bank and made cashier Thomas G. Ayres and his force put $20,240 in their bag while at the Condon bank, but $3,000 were secured, as Cashier C. M. Ball told them the time lock was on.

Bob and Emmett were the first to finish their work, and, forcing Mr. Ayers, his son Bert, and teller Shepherd out in front of them, they emerged from the door to be met by two shots from George Cubine and C. S. Cox. Turning, the Daltons ran back through the bank while the robbers in Condon & Co.'s bank across the street fired, fatally wounding cashier Ayres. Bob and Emmett, running around from the back, found Lucius Baldwin, whom they shot. Coming out in front on Eighth Street, they fired another volley, killing Cubine and fatally wounding Charles Brown, a shoemaker. Both then fired at Cox, and the bullets whistled all around him, but he miraculously escaped.

The two Daltons joined the rest of the gang and started for their horses, which were hitched in the alley just west of the Condon bank. Before they reached them, they were downed by bullets from rifles in the hands of determined citizens, but not before Bob Dalton killed city marshal C. T. Connelly.

All the money was recovered and turned over to the bank. Baldwin and Brown died this evening. Emmett Dalton is badly hurt and has made a statement, acknowledging his identity and identifying all of the gang. He says that Bob and Grat were in the California robbery for which they were wanted and also executed the express robbery at Adair some weeks ago. This is the Dalton boys' old home, and they were well-known by all old citizens.

DETAILS OF THE AFFAIR

COFFEYVILLE, Kan., Oct. 5. The Dalton gang has been exterminated, wiped off the face of the earth. Caught like rats in a trap, they were today shot down, but not until four citizens of this place had yielded up their lives in the work of extermination. Six of the gang rode into town this morning and robbed two banks of this place. Their coming had become known to the officers of the law, and when the bandits attempted to escape, they were attacked by the marshal's pose. In the battle which ensued, four of the desperadoes were killed outright, and one was so fatally wounded that he has since died. The other escaped but is being hotly pursued. Of the attacking party, four were killed, one was fatally, and two were seriously wounded.

The dead are as follows:

- Bob Dalton, desperado, shot through the head.
- Gratton Dalton, desperado, shot through the heart.
- Emmett Dalton, desperado, shot through the left side. [The paper was wrong here. Emmett survived the shooting.]
- Joseph Evans, desperado, shot through the head.
- John Moore ("Texas Jack"), desperado, shot through the head.
- C. T. Connelly, city marshal, shot through the body.
- E. M. Baldwin, bank clerk, shot through the head.
- G. V. Cubine, merchant, shot through the head.
- C. J. Brown, shoemaker, shot through the body.

- Thomas G. Ayers, cashier of the First National Bank, was shot through the groin and cannot live.
- T. A. Reynolds of the attacking party has a wound in the right breast, but it is not considered necessarily dangerous.
- Louis Dietz, another member of the attacking party, was shot in the right side. His wound is a serious one but is not fatal.

It had been rumored a month ago that the Dalton gang had been contemplating an immediate raid upon the banks of this city. Arrangements were made to give them a warm reception, and for over a week, a patrol was maintained night and day to give warning of the gang's approach. The raid did not take place, and then came the report from Deming, N. M., that the United States officers had had a battle with the band in that territory and that three of the bandits had been killed. This report was believed here to have been circulated by the Daltons themselves, the intention being to divert attention from their real movements and to lull the people of the town into a sense of security. The people, however, were not so easily deceived, and when the report of the disaster to the gang in New Mexico was denied, vigilance was renewed. Still, the expected raid was not made, and finally, the patrol was withdrawn last Saturday, although every stranger was carefully scrutinized as soon as he appeared on the streets.

THE ARRIVAL OF THE GANG

It was 9 o'clock this morning when the Dalton gang rode into town. They came in two squads of three each and, passing through unfrequented streets and deserted alleys, rendezvoused in the alley in the rear of the First National Bank. They quickly tied their horses and, without losing a moment's time, proceeded to the attack upon the banks. Robert Dalton, the notorious leader of the gang, and Emmett, his brother, went to the First National Bank. The other four, under the leadership of "Texas Jack" or John Moore, going to the private bank of C. M. Condon & Co. In the meantime, the alarm had been given. The Dalton boys were born and bred in this vicinity and were well known to nearly every man, woman, and child in the town, and in their progress, through the town, they had been recognized.

    City Marshal Connelly was quickly notified of their arrival, and almost before the bandits had entered the banks, he was collecting a posse to capture them if possible, to kill them if necessary. He ran first to the livery stable of Jim Spears—a dead shot with a Winchester and a valuable man in any fight. Then he summoned George Cubine, a merchant; Charles Brown, a shoemaker; John Cox, the express agent, and other citizens who could be conveniently reached. Stationing them about the square which both banks faced, he hastened to augment his posse by summoning other citizens for impromptu police duty. While the marshal was collecting his forces, the bandits, all ignorant of the trap that was being laid for them, were proceeding deliberately with their work of robbing the banks.

AT THE BANKS

"Texas Jack's" band had entered the Condon bank and, with their Winchesters leveled at cashier Bail, and teller Carpenter had ordered them to throw up their hands. Then "Texas Jack" searched them for weapons while the other three desperadoes kept them covered with their rifles. Finding them to be unarmed, cashier Ball was ordered to open the safe. The cashier explained that the safe's door was controlled by a time lock and that it could not by any means short of dynamite be opened before its time was up, which would be 10 o'clock or in about twenty minutes.

"We'll wait," said the leader, and he sat down at the cashier's desk.

"How about the money drawer?" he asked suddenly, and, jumping up, he walked around to the cages of the paying and receiving tellers and, taking the money, amounting in all to less than $300, dumped it into a flour sack with which he was supplied, and again sat down while the time lock slowly ticked off the seconds and the hands of the clock tardily moved toward the hour of 10 o'clock.

Bob and Emmett Dalton, in the meantime, were having better luck at the First National Bank. When they entered the bank, they found within cashier Ayers, and his son Albert Ayers, and teller W. H. Shepherd. None of them were armed, and with leveled revolvers, the bandits easily intimidated them. Albert Ayers and teller Shepherd were kept under the muzzles of Emmett Dalton's revolvers while Bob Dalton forced cashier Ayers to strip the safe vault and cash drawer of all the money contained in them and place it in a sack which had been brought along for that purpose. Fearing to leave them behind lest they should give the alarm before the bandits should be able to mount their horses and escape, the desperadoes marched the officers of the bank out of the doors with the intention of keeping them under guard while they made their escape. The party made its appearance at the door of the bank just as liveryman Spears and his companions of the marshal's posse took their positions in the square.

When the Dalton brothers saw the armed men in the square, they appreciated their peril on the instant, and leaving the bank officers on the steps of the bank building; they ran for their horses. As soon as they reached the sidewalk, Spears' rifle quickly came into position. An instant later, it spoke, and Bob Dalton, the notorious leader of the notorious gang, fell in his tracks, dead. There was not the quiver of a muscle after he fell. The bullet had struck him in the right temple and plowed through the brain, and passed out just above the left eye. Emmett Dalton had the start of his brother, and before Spears could draw a bead on him, he had dodged behind the corner of the bank building and was making time in the direction of the alley where the bandits had tied their horses.

The shot which dropped Bob Dalton aroused "Texas Jack's" band in the Condon bank, who were yet patiently waiting for the time lock of the safe to be sprung with the hour of tea. Raising their rifles to their shoulders, they fired one volley out of the windows. Two men fell at the volley. Cashier Ayers fell on the steps of his bank, shot through the groin, and shoemaker Brown of the attacking party in the square was shot through the body. Brown was quickly removed to his shop but died just as he was carried within. The firing attracted the attention of marshal Connelly, who was collecting more men for his posse, and with the few which he had already gathered, he ran hurriedly to the scene of conflict.

After firing their volley from the windows of the bank the bandits, appreciating that their only safety lay in flight, attempted to escape. They ran from the rear of the bank, firing as they fled. The marshal's posse in the square, without organization of any kind, fired at the fleeing bandits, each man for himself. Spears' Winchester spoke twice more in quick succession before the others of the posse could take aim, and Joseph Evans and "Texas Jack" fell dead, both shot through the head, making three dead bandits to his credit. In the general fusillade Grat Dalton, one of the two surviving members of "Texas Jack's" squad, and Marshal Connelly and George Cubine were mortally hit and died on the field, and Lin Baldwin, one of Condon's clerks, who was out collecting when the attack was made. Allie Ogee, the only surviving member of "Texas Jack's" squad, successfully escaped to the alley where the horses were tied and, mounting the swiftest horse of the lot, fled south in the direction of the Indian territory.

Emmett Dalton, who had escaped from the First National Bank, had already reached the alley in safety, but he had some trouble in getting mounted, and Allie Ogee had already made his escape before Emmett got fairly started. Several of the posse, anticipating that horses would be required, were mounted and quickly pursued the escaping bandits. Emmett Dalton's horse was no match for the fresher animals of his pursuers. As his pursuers closed on him, he turned suddenly in his saddle and fired upon his would-be captors. The latter answered with a volley, and Emmett toppled from his horse hard hit. He was brought back to town and died late this afternoon. [Editor's note: Emmett was seriously wounded but managed to survive—despite the odds]. He made an antemortem statement, confessed to various crimes committed by the gang of which he was a member. Allie Ogee had about ten minutes the start of his pursuers and was mounted on a swift horse. At 5 o'clock this evening, he had not been captured.

AFTER THE BATTLE

After the battle was over, a search was made for the money which the bandits had secured from the two banks. It was found in the sacks where it had been placed by the robbers. One sack was found under the body of Bob Dalton, who had fallen dead upon it while he was escaping from the First National Bank. The other was found tightly clutched in "Texas Jack's" hand. The money was restored to its rightful owners. The bodies of those of the attacking party who were killed were taken to their respective homes, while the bodies of the dead bandits were allowed to remain where they had fallen until the arrival of the coroner from Independence, who ordered them removed to the courthouse. There he held an inquest, the jury returning a verdict in accordance with the facts. The inquest over the bodies of the dead citizens will be postponed until the result of the pursuit of Allie Ogee is known.

During the time the bodies remained in the square, they were viewed by hundreds of people of this and surrounding towns, who, having heard of the tragedy, came in swarms to inspect the scene. The excitement was of the most intense character, and the fate of Allie Ogee, should he be captured, was determined by universal consent. He will be hanged by the people. Other topics which attracted universal comment were the fulfillment of the prophecy that the Daltons would "die with their boots on," the peculiar fate which had decreed that they should die by the hands of their old friends in the vicinity of their birthplace, and the excellent marksmanship of liveryman Spears, who, with three shots, sent death to as many bandits.

OGEE BADLY WANTED

Up to 10 o'clock tonight, Allie Ogee had not been captured—at least, it is not known that he has been. The pursuing party is still out, and it is believed that they are still following the bandit's trail. Ogee had such a short start that it is not believed that he will be able to escape. He, however, is well acquainted with the country south of here in the Indian Territory where the bandits had their headquarters. It may be that he can thus elude his pursuers.

The capture of Ogee is particularly desirable because he being the only surviving member of the gang, is believed to be the only person who knows the hiding place of the great treasure which they have accumulated during the years of their outlawry. They could not have spent all their ill-gotten money even if they had lived among the luxuries of civilization. As it was, they were hiding during the greater part of their criminal career and have had no opportunity to spend the money. The location of the treasure is, therefore, a matter of great interest, and it is believed that Ogee can be made to reveal it if he is caught. This phase of the case has only just now presented itself to the people here, and it doubtless had not occurred to Ogee's pursuers at all. It is believed that in their excitement and indignation, they will take summary vengeance upon him before ascertaining from him where the treasure is hidden.

EMMETT YET ALIVE

Emmett Dalton is not dead. He is slowly dying in a room at a hotel here, and his death is expected at any moment. The indignation against the robbers became so intense this afternoon that the citizens wanted to lynch the dying bandit. To prevent this, the coroner gave out a statement that he was already dead. This delayed the excitement, and now the people will wait for death to do the work that they had planned should be done by lynch law.

Emmett Dalton is being closely guarded by a company of citizens tonight under command of the deputy city marshal. Only newspaper correspondents are admitted to see him. The Associated Press representative saw him at 11 o'clock tonight and procured from him a statement of his life, particular question being paid to the last two years of it.

He confessed that the gang was responsible for the Red Rock, Wharton, Adair, and all train robberies in the Indian Territory, which had been credited to them. The story of hidden treasure, he said, was nonsense.

"If there had been treasure," he said, "we would all have been alive today. It was because we were all broke that we planned the Coffeyville raid. We were being hard-pressed by the officers in the territory and thought that we would have to get out of the country. We planned the robbery about two weeks ago while we were camped in the Osage country."

"Bob said we would outdo the James boys' exploits and would go to Coffeyville and raid both banks at the same time. We tried to persuade him not to do it, and then he called us cowards, that settled it, and we started for the scene of the raid. We all met Monday night at Tulsa and proceeded by easy stages to Timber Hill, twelve miles north of here, when we stopped last night. We started for

Coffeyville at 6:30 o'clock this morning and arrived here about 9.30 o'clock. You know the rest."

It was with great difficulty that the bandit told his story, as he was suffering terrible agony from a wound in the side. The physician attending him says that he cannot possibly survive.

Cashier Ayers, who is suffering from a wound in the groin, is resting easier tonight, but his condition is still critical.

At 11 o'clock, nothing had been heard of the party in pursuit of Allie Ogee.

The reward for the capture of the Daltons or the delivery of their bodies to the officer of the law are estimated to amount to $12,000—offered by the Southern Pacific, the Missouri Pacific, the Frisco, the Missouri, Kansas, and Texas, and the Santa Fe. If these rewards are collected, it is hoped that they will be turned over to the families of those citizens who lost their lives in today's battle.

CAREER OF THE DALTONS

The Daltons were a numerous family. There were five boys and three girls. Of the boys, two are engaged in farming— one in Oklahoma, where the mother of the family lives, and one near Coffeyville, where three of the brothers met their death today. The Daltons were second cousins of the noted

James boys, who defied the law in Missouri for so many years, and through them were, related to the Youngers, who are now serving life terms of imprisonment in the penitentiary of Minnesota.

Bob Dalton was the first of the boys to enter upon a career of crime. While he was scarcely more than a boy, he became a cattle thief and did a thriving business in driving off cattle from the herds on the Cherokee strip and taking them across the Indian Territory into Colorado, where he would sell them. He was joined soon after he entered the business by his brother, Gratton Dalton. Their depredations became so frequent and troublesome that the cattlemen organized to drive them from the strip. A posse of cowboys was formed for that purpose and gave the Daltons a hard chase, finally losing them in the wilds of New Mexico.

The next heard of the Daltons was in California, where they took to train and stage robbery. While robbing a stage there, one of the passengers was killed in the attack. This spurred the officers on to extraordinary efforts to effect the capture of the gang, and Grat Dalton was finally captured. While being taken to a place for safekeeping, he was rescued by the other members of the gang, the whole party finally escaping, after being chased out of California and through a good part of Arizona.

In the spring of 1889, the gang turned up again in the Indian Territory, and when Oklahoma was opened to settlement, the Dalton boys secured a choice claim for their mother near Kingfisher, where she lives, supported by one of her sons. At the time of the opening, Bob Dalton was made United States deputy marshal, being selected on account of his peculiar fitness to deal with desperate characters. After the opening, he returned to his life of outlawry, and he and Grat were then joined by their brother Emmett, the youngest of the brothers. They were at that time also joined by "Texas Jack" and soon gathered about them several more desperate characters.

It was then that the most successful period of the Daltons' career, from their standpoint, began. Their attention was first directed to the robbery of express trains, and they perpetrated many successful "hold-ups," the most noted of which are the robberies of the Santa Fe at Wharton, the Missouri Pacific at Adair, and the Frisco near Vinita.

The Wharton robbery was perhaps the most dramatic of all. The robber went to Wharton on horseback and, entering the station there, asked the operator to find out if the train was on time. He replied that he would do so when one of the band, fearing that the operator had recognized them, shot him dead upon the spot without word of warning. When the train arrived, it was held up after the regular manner.

In the pursuit of the robbers which followed, Charles Bryant was captured at Hennessey by deputy United States Marshal Short, known throughout the territory as a most-brave officer. Short placed his captive in the baggage car of the Rock Island train to take him to the Wichita jail. He had disarmed and ironed Bryant, and receiving an intimation that the gang would attempt to rescue Bryant at Wakomus, a small station in the Cherokee strip, he placed his captive in the charge of the baggage master, giving the baggage man his (Short's) revolver. When the station was reached, Short got off to see if any of the gang were around but seeing none, he got on again. When he reached the car, Bryant had secured one of the weapons and, holding it in one of his manacled hands, fired, mortally wounding Short. The officer had the strength to seize a Winchester and pump four bullets into Bryant's body, expiring as he pulled the trigger the last time.

The Adair robbery resulted in the death of two men. The express car was guarded on that occasion, and a hot fight took place between the guards and the robbers. The place where the train was held up was in the midst of the town. One stray bullet passed into the room of a physician and, striking the doctor in the head, killed him instantly. Another physician, who, hearing the firing, had run in its direction, was also shot and killed.

The last train robbery of the gang was of the Frisco near Vinita. The amount secured by the robbers in their various raids will probably never be known. It was very great, however, and has been estimated at $300,000. After the Frisco robbery, the Daltons seemed to have devoted their attention to the robbery of banks. Today's was the last raid of the gang, and with it ended, the existence of a band equaled only in the desperate character of its undertakings by the James and Younger band.

Nick Vulich

About This Book

This is no ordinary history book. It's a contemporary history – written almost entirely from frontier newspaper accounts. Because of this, the facts may not all be dead on. Some dates or events may be a bit iffy or a little off. I acknowledge when the account quoted differs from the currently accepted version of the story.

Frontier journalists were quick to tell a story but somewhat lax in performing fact-checks.

In the case of "Dynamite Dick," every time a paper reported one of his many deaths, they called him by a different name—other than Dan Clifton. I don't know how many accounts I read about street fights, or running fights with posses, as the robbers made their escapes. Several accounts would say ten or fifteen shots were fired; another journalist would take liberties with the story, telling how hundreds of rounds were flung back and forth, lead flying hot and heavy through the air.

Blood and gore were a favorite of frontier journalists. Many would take great pains to describe dead bodies, bullet wounds, and the look on the face of a dead bandit in great detail. When the *San Francisco Chronicle* detailed Black Jack Ketchum's botched hanging, they wrote, "When the body dropped through the trap, the half-inch rope severed the head as cleanly as if a knife had cut it." After the Dalton brother's fateful raid at Coffeyville, a report said, "whenever Grat Dalton's right arm was lifted, a little spurt of blood would jump from the round black hole in his throat."

That's what I like best about early newspaper accounts. They give you the flavor of the event. They let you know what people were thinking, what they were feeling.

I'm going to be brutally honest here. A lot of people don't like the way I write history. They say my books are short on interpretation, and long on description, meaning I'm concentrated more on telling the story than on why it happened, what it means, and what could have or should have happened.

My answer to that is I'd rather sell the sizzle.

The story is what's important to me. I want to watch it unravel, all fast and furious like. I jump from event to event, from train robbery to bank robbery to the gang being shot all to hell by the posse.

There's no stopping.

There is no slowing down to examine the whys, the wheres, the what ifs, the could have beens, and the should have beens. Those things were irrelevant to the outlaws.

They were hell-bent on beating it out of town without getting shot full of holes, of staying two steps ahead of the pursuing posse.

If they stopped for even a moment to think or reflect on events, they would have been plugged full of lead or left swinging from the nearest branch.

Taking a moment to think things through wasn't a luxury most robbers or posses had. Instead, they were engaged in a no holds barred battle - one to escape and enjoy the fruits of their robbery, the other to bring the outlaws back to justice or see them strung up from the nearest tree branch.

Lives were on the line. Lead flowed freely, and most outlaws faced a shorter-than-average life expectancy no matter how smart or lucky.

That's the story I want to tell.

About the Author

Nick Vulich usually writes short, easy-to-read solutions to your e-commerce problems, but now and then, he likes to return to his roots: historical writing.

This book is a collection of short *historical vignettes*. Some debunk popular myths, talk about little-known historical events, or approach well-known events from a different perspective.

Everything in this book is true. No names have been changed to protect the innocent—or guilty. Any conversation included within quotes is authentic and taken from contemporary sources. I've tried my hardest to stick to the facts. Many times, it's nearly impossible to distinguish truth from fiction because there are so many competing accounts. I've tried to stick with the version the experts "say" is accurate in those cases. I understand—there are at least two sides to every story. Some readers will disagree with my choices, and that's the way it should be. History is fluid. We reinterpret the facts from generation to generation.

Remember, there are two sides to every story, and what you believe depends on your perspective.

December 5, 2022
Nick Vulich
Clinton, Iowa

Bibliography

Alexander, General E. P. "Pickett's Charge and Artillery Fighting at Gettysburg." *The Century Magazine* January 1887: 464 - 471.

Alexander, H. H. *The Life of Guiteau and the Official History of ... the Trial of the Guiteau For Assassinating Pres. Garfield*. 1882.

Ambrose, Stephen E. *Crazy Horse, and Custer: The Parallel Lives of Two American Warriors*. 2012.

Anderson, Rasmus B. *The Norse Discovery of America*. 1906.

Anonymous. *Life and Adventures of Sam Bass: The Notorious Union Pacific and Texas Train Robber*. 1878.

Armstrong, Perry A. *The Sauks and the Black Hawk War with Biographical Sketches, etc.* 1887.

Baker, Pearl. *The Wild Bunch at Robbers Roost*. 1989.

Balderston, George Canby, and Lloyd. *The Evolution of the American Flag*. 1909.

Blue, Corinne J. Naden and Rose. *Belle Starr and the Wild West*. 2000.

Boorman, Dean K. *Guns of the Old West: An Illustrated History*. 2004.

Brackenridge, Hugh Henry. *Incidents of the Insurrection in the Western Parts of Pennsylvania, in the Year 1794*. n.d.

Buchanan, James. *Mr. Buchanan's Administration on the Eve of the Rebellion*. 1866.

Buel, J. W. *Heroes of the Plains, or Lives and Wonderful Adventures of Wild Bill, Buffalo Bill, Kit Carson, Capt. Payne, "White Beaver," Capt. Jack, Texas Jack, California Joe, and Other Celebrated Indian Fighters, Scouts, Hunters, and Guides*. 1891.

—. *Life and Marvelous Adventures of Wild Bill the Scout*. 1880.

—. *The Border Outlaws*. 1884.

Buel, James W. *The Border Outlaws: An authentic and thrilling history of the most noted bandits of ancient and modern times: the Younger brothers, Jesse and Frank James, and their comrades in crime*. 1881.

Burton, Jeffrey. *The Deadliest Outlaws: The Ketchum Gang and the Wild Bunch*. 2009.

—. *The Deadliest Outlaws: The Ketchum Gang and the Wild Bunch*. 2009.

Calhoun, John C. *The South Carolina Exposition*. 1832.

Carlson, Chip. *Tom Horn: Blood on the Moon*. 2001.

Carr, Harry. "The Bandits and the Buried Gold of El Tejon." *The Yale Expositor* 21 August 1913.

Carrington, Henry B. *Battles of the American Revolution, 1775 - 1781: Historical and Military Criticism with Topographical Illustration*. 1876.

Casas, Bartolomé de las. *A Brief Account of the Destruction of the Indies*. 1561.

Chapman, Arthur. "Lively Days in Dodge City With Bat Masterson." *New York Tribune* 6 November 1921: 4.

Comegys, Jack. "The Gentle Art of Train Robbery." *Shield's Magazine* Novemeber 1905: 449-453.

Cooke, Tim. *Butch Cassidy and the Sundance Kid: Notorious Outlaws of the West*. 2016.

Crawford, Captain Jack. "The Truth About Calamity Jane." *The Journalist*. 5 March 1904.

Dacus, J. A. *Illustrated Lives and Adventures of Frank and Jesse James and the Younger Brothers - The Noted Outlaws*. 1881.

DeArment, Robert K. *Alias Frank Canton*. 1996.

DeMattos, Jack and Parsons, Chuck. *The Notorious Luke Short: Sporting Man of the Wild West*. 2015.

Donald, Jay. *Outlaws of the Border: A Complete and Authentic History of the Lives of Frank and Jesse James and Their Robber Companions, Including Quantrell and His Noted Guerillas*. 1883.

Dykstra, Robert R. *The Cattle Towns*. 1983.

Estleman, Loren D. *Aces, and Eights: The Legend of Wild Bill Hickok*. 2010.

Etulain, Richard W. *The Life and Legends of Calamity Jane*. 2014.

Frothingham, Richard. *Battle of Bunker Hill*. 1890.

Gardner, Mark Lee. *Shot All to Hell: Jesse James, the Northfield Raid, and the Wild West's Greatest Escape*. 2013.

—. *To Hell on a Fast Horse: Billy the Kid, Pat Garrett, and the Epic Chase to Justice in the Old West*. 2010.

Garland, Hamlin. "Custer's Last Fight As Seen By Two Moon." *McClure's Magazine* September 1898: 443 - 448.

Garrett, Pat. *The Authentic Life of Billy the Kid*. 1882.

Gillett, James B. *Six Years With the Texas Rangers*. 1921, n.d.

Haley, W. D. "Johnny Appleseed - A Pioneer Hero." *Harper's New Monthly Magazine* November 1871: 830-837.

Hardin, John Wesley. *The Life of John Wesley Hardin*. 1896.

Harman, S. W. *Hell On the Border*. 1898.

Hatch, Thom. *The Last Outlaws: Butch Cassidy and the Sundance Kid*. 2013.

Hayey, Henry Gillespie. *A Complete History of the Life and Trial of Charles Julius Guiteau, Assassin of President Garfield*. 1882.

Hensel, W. U. *Buchanan's Administration on the Eve of the Rebellion*. 1908.

Herring, Hal. *Famous Firearms of the Old West: From Wild Bill Hickok's Colt Revolvers to Geronimo's Winchester, Twelve Guns That Shaped Our History*. 2011.

Hewes, George R. T. *Traits of the Tea Party*. 1835.

Hoeper, George. *Black Bart: Boulevardier Bandit*. 1995.

Hogeland, William. *The Whiskey Rebellion: George Washington, Alexander Hamilton, and Frontier Rebels Who Challenged America's Newfound Sovereignty*. 2010.

Holland, Henry W. *William Dawes and His Ride with Paul Revere*. 1878.

Horan, James David. *Desperate Men: The James Gang and the Wild Bunch*. 1962.

Hudd, Alfred E. *Richard Ameryk and the Name America*. 1910.

Hudd, Alfred E. "Richard Ameryk and the name America." *Proceedings of the Clifton Antiquarian Club* 1909 - 1910: 8 - 24.

Hunt, General Henry J. "The Battle of the First Day at Gettysburg." *The Century Magazine* November 1886: 112 - 133.

—. "The Second Day at Gettysburg." *The Century Magazine* December 1886: 278 - 296.

—. "The Third Day at Gettysburg." *The Century Magazine* January 1887: 451 -464.

Jane, Calamity. *The Life and Adventures of Calamity Jane*. 1896.

John Mitchinson, John Lloyd. *The Book of General Ignorance*. 2006.

Jucovy, Linda. *Searching for Calamity Jane: The Life and Times of Calamity Jane*. 2012.

Jung, Patrick J. *The Black Hawk War of 1832*. 2008.

Kearns, Doris. *Team of Rivals: The Political Genius of Abraham Lincoln*. 2006.

Kelly, Charles. *The Outlaw Trail: A History of Butch Cassidy and His Wild Bunch*. 1996.

Krakel, Dean. *The Saga of Tom Horn*. 1954.

Law, General E. M. "Round Top and the Confederate Right at Gettysburg." *The Century Magazine* December 1886: 296 - 306.

Levene, William Collins, and Bruce. *Black Bart: The True Story of the West's Most Famous Stage Coach Robber*. 1992.

Lossing, Benson J. *The Pictorial Field Book of the Revolution (2 Volumes)*. 1860.

MacKell, Jan. *Red Light Women of the Rocky Mountains*. 2011.

Masterson, Bat. *Famous Gunfighters of the Western Frontier*. 1959.

Maynard, Nettie Colburn. *Was Abraham Lincoln a Spiritualist?* 1891.

McGinnis, Bruce. *Reflections in Dark Glass: The Life and Times of John Wesley Hardin*. 1996.

McLaird, James D. *Calamity Jane: The Woman and the Legend*. 2005.

—. "Calamity Jane: The Life and Legend." *South Dakota History* 1994.

Miller, Floyd. *Bill Tilghman, Marshal of the Last Frontier*. 1968.

Moore, Frederick. "How Buffalo Bill Won His Name." *The Wide World Magazine* May 1903: 42 - 47.

Morgan, Robert. *Lions of the West: Heroes and Villains of the Westward Expansion*. 2012.

Nash, Jay Robert. *Encyclopedia of Western Lawmen and Outlaws*. 1992.

Nichols, George Ward. "Wild Bill." *Harper's New Monthly Magazine* February 1867.

O'Donoghue, Denis. *The Voyage of St Brendan the Abbot*. 1893.

O'Neal, Bill. *Encyclopedia of Western Gunfighters*. 1991.

Patterson, W. G. "Calamity Jane A Heroine of the Wild West." *The Wide World Magazine* September 1903: 450 - 457.

Penrose, Charles. *The Rustler Business*. 1982.

Prentiss Ingraham, M. D. Ruggles, and Edward P. Doherty. "Pursuit and Death of John Wilkes Booth." *The Century Magazin*. January 1890. P. 443 - 449.

Ridge, John Rollin. "The Life and Adventures of Joaquin Murrieta." 1854.

—. *The Life and Adventures of Joaquin Murrieta*. 1854.

Roberts, Gary L. *Doc Holliday: The Life and Legend*. 2011.

Rosa, Joseph G. *The Gunfighter: Man or Myth*. 1979.

—. *Wild Bill Hickok: The Man and His Myth*. 1996.

Saint-Germain, C. de. *The Dalton Brothers and Their Astounding Career of Crime*. 1892.

Scott, Richard. *Eyewitness to the Old West: Firsthand Account of Exploration, Adventure, and Peril*. 2002.

Severin, Timothy. *The Brendan Voyage*. 2010.

Shillingberg, William B. *Dodge City: The Early Years, 1872 - 1886*. 2009.

Shirley, Glenn. *Belle Star: The Literature, The Facts, and The Legend*. 2014.

—. *Heck Thomas, Frontier Marshal*. 1962.

Simmons, Marc. *When Six-Guns Ruled: Outlaw Tales of the Southwest*. 1990.

Siringo, Charles. *History of Billy the Kid*. 1920.

Slaughter, Thomas P. *The Whiskey Rebellion: Frontier Epilogue to the American Revolution*. 1988.

Smith, John. *General Historie of Virginia*. 1632.

Smith, Robert Barr. *Outlaw Women: The Wild West's Most Notorious Daughters, Wives, and Mothers*. 2015.

—. *The Outlaws: Tales of Bad Guys Who Shaped the Wild West*. 2013.

Souter, Gerry, and Souter, Janet. *Guns of Outlaws: Weapons of the American Bad Man*. 2014.

Spangenberger, Phil. "Hardin's Deadly Tools: John Wesley Hardin was a master craftsman of death, and these were the tools of his trade." *True West* 12 March 2012.

Spurr, Howard W. *The Paul Revere Album*. 1903.

Staff, Editorial. "An Arizona Episode." *Cosmopolitan Magazine* October 1899.

Stanley, F. *No Tears For Black Jack Ketchum*. 2008.

Stevens, Frank Everett. *The Black Hawk War*. 1903.

Stiles, T. J. *Jesse James: Last Rebel of the Civil War*. 2010.

Sturges, J. A. *Illustrated History of McDonald County, Missouri: From the Earliest Settlement to the Present Time*. 1897.

Swaney, Burton T. Hoyle and Homer H. *Lives of James A. Garfield and Chester A. Arthur with a Brief History of the Assassin*. 1881.

Swett, S. *History of the Bunker Hill Battle with a Plan*. 1826.

Thatcher, John Boyd. *Christopher Columbus: His Life, His Work, His Remains*. 1904.

Thwaites, Reuben Gold. *The Story of the Black Hawk War*. 1892.

Tilghman, Zoe A. "My Husband Helped Tame the West." *Life Magazine* 18 May 1959.

Tilghman, Zoe Agnes Stratton. *Marshal of the Last Frontier: Life and Services of William Matthew (Bill) Tilghman*. 1949.

Townsend, George Aldred. *The Life Crimes and Capture of John Wilkes Booth*. 1865.

Townsend, George Alfred. "How Wilkes Booth Crossed the Potomac." *The Century Magazine* April 1884: 822 -832.

Tripp, C. A. *The Intimate World of Abraham Lincoln*. 2006.

Varigny, C. De. *The Women of the United States*. 1895.

Vespucci, Amerigo. *Mundus Novus Letter to Lorenzo Pietro Di Medici*. 1916.

Wakefield, John Allen. *History of the Black Hawk War*. 1856.

Weik, Jesse W. "A New Story of Lincoln's Assassination." *The Century Magazine* February 1913: 559 - 562.

White, Jack. *Preacherman's Son: Gunfighter John Wesley Hardin*. 2014.

Williams, Michael. "Real Men Stories of Arizona." *Pearson's Magazine* February 1913: 148-154.

Williamson, G. R. *Frontier Gambling*. 2012.

—. *Frontier Gambling: The Games, the Gamblers & the Great Gambling Halls of the Old West*. 2011.

Wilson, Gary A. *Tiger of the Wild Bunch: The Life and Death of Harvey "Kid Curry" Logan*. 2007.

Wilson, Michael R. *Great Stagecoach Robberies of the Old West*. 2007.

Newspapers Consulted

Abbeville Press and Banner (Abbeville, South Carolina)

Albuquerque Morning Journal

Anaconda Standard (Anaconda, Montana)

Arizona Daily Star (Tucson, Arizona)

Arizona Republican

Arizona Weekly Citizen

Atchison Daily Champion

Austin Weekly Statesman

Barbour County Index (Medicine Lodge, Kansas)

Black Hills Daily Times (Deadwood City, Dakota Territory)

Butler Weekly Times (Butler, Missouri)

Butte Inter Mountain (Butte, Montana)

Cheyenne Daily Leader

Chickasha Daily Express (Chickasha, Indian Territory)

Coffeyville Journal (Coffeyville, Kansas)

Daily Ardmoreite (Ardmore, Oklahoma Territory)

Dallas Daily Herald

Dallas Morning News

Dallas Weekly Herald

Dodge City Times

Dillon Tribune (Dillon, Montana)

El Paso Times

Evening Bulletin (Maysville, Kansas)
Fort Worth Daily Gazette
Galveston Daily News
Guthrie Daily Leader
Havre Herald (Havre, Montana)
Herald Democrat
Houston Daily Post
Junction City Union (Junction City, Kansas)
Kalispell Bee (Kalispell, Montana)
Leavenworth Times
Mexico Weekly Ledger (Mexico, Missouri)
Minneapolis Journal
Mower County Transcript (Lansing, Michigan)
Neihart Herald (Neihart, Montana)
New York Herald
New York Times
New York Tribune
Omaha Daily Bee
Pensacola Journal
Public Ledger (Memphis, Tennessee)
Red Lodge Pickett (Red Lodge, Montana)
Rosebud County News (Forsyth, Montana)
Saint Paul Globe
Salt Lake Herald
Salt Lake Tribune
San Francisco Call

San Francisco Chronicle
San Francisco Examiner
Seattle Post intelligencer
Sedalia Weekly Bazoo (Sedalia, Missouri)
Spokane Press
St. Landry Democrat (Opelousas, Louisiana)
St. Louis Globe-Democrat
The Evening Statesman (Walla Walla, Washington)
The Globe Republican (Dodge City, Kansas)
The Times (Washington, DC)
The Yale Expositor (St. Clair County, Missouri)
Topeka State Journal
Washington Times
Watchman and Southron (Sumter, South Carolina)
Western Kansas World
Wheeling Daily Intelligencer (Wheeling, West Virginia)
Wichita Daily Eagle
Yorkville Enquirer

Made in United States
North Haven, CT
13 June 2023